Confronting Bullying
Literacy as a Tool for Character Education

Roxanne Henkin

HEINEMANN
Portsmouth, NH

To my family

Our families play important roles in promoting literacy, helping us develop the courage and fortitude to deal with life, and
confronting bullying, violence, and harassment in our
schools. Teachers and schools, parents and families all need
to work together to build a safer world for our children.

And to Mary Lou Daugherty, who makes everything
possible.

Heinemann
A division of Reed Elsevier Inc.
361 Hanover Street
Portsmouth, NH 03801–3912
www.heinemann.com

Offices and agents throughout the world

© 2005 by Roxanne Henkin

Library of Congress Cataloging-in-Publication Data
Henkin, Roxanne.
    Confronting bullying : literacy as a tool for character education / Roxanne
Henkin.
        p. cm.
    Includes bibliographical references.
    ISBN 0-325-00413-7 (alk. paper)
    1. Bullying in schools—Prevention. 2. Language arts (Elementary).
3. Moral education. I. Title.
LB3013.3.H45 2005
371.5'8—dc22   2004023992

Editor: Leigh Peake
Production editor: Sonja S. Chapman
Cover design: Jenny Jensen Greenleaf
Compositor: Valerie Levy/Drawing Board Studios
Manufacturing: Steve Bernier

Printed in the United States of America on acid-free paper
09 08 07 06 05   DA   2   3   4   5

Contents

Acknowledgments

No book has ever been written alone, and this one is no exception. This book is based on my research, much of which has been done in conjunction with Dr. Lorri Davis. We have worked together, taught together, analyzed research and come up with new theoretical insights together. I thank her and I treasure our collaboration.

I also want to thank Jerome Harste for his support and insight, and his research, which has always been cutting edge and theory building. I also want to thank Debra Goodman, William Spurlin, James Sullivan, Rose Casement, Hannah Furrow, and Kathy Egawa for our endless conversations about teaching and social justice, and their critiques on my work.

I am indebted to the critical literacy researchers and the effect their research has had on my thinking. I especially want to thank Lorraine Wilson, Vivian Vasquez, Alan Luke, Peter Freebody, Barbara Comber, and Hilary Janks for their work in this field.

I also want to thank my colleagues in the Reading and Language Program of National-Louis University in Chicago for their support and insights into my work during my time there. Thank you Camille Blachowicz, Jeanne Chaney, Peter Fisher, Ken Kantor, Susan McMahon, Donna Ogle, and Junko Yokota. I also want to thank Becky Barr whose early death broke all our hearts. And I want to thank all my new colleagues at The University of Texas San Antonio. Our shared interest and work with diversity has enriched this book.

Many of the ideas in this book came from the work I did in conjunction with The Illinois Language and Literacy Council. We offered summer workshops with teachers that focused on using literacy to confront bullying. I want to thank the doctoral students and the other teachers who worked so hard especially for the annual Illinois Young Authors Conference. Many thanks to Susan Anderson, Gwen Zolezzi, Rosalie Musiola, Dennis Szymkowiak, Chris Poziemski, Jean-Louise Gustafson, Sharon Ball, Faith Mirza, Doris Aimers, Ruth Stevik, Julie Milos, Krissy Strong, Meg Pyterek, and Jeff Siddall. A special thanks to Jan Dundon who shared her amazing knowledge of books with all of us at our conferences.

I want to thank the many teachers who so graciously opened up their classrooms to me. I want to especially thank Mickey Nuccio, Peggy Nadziejko, Ginger Weincek, and Kathleen Jesuskaitis for allowing me into their classroom lives. Their fine teaching and reflections made this book possible. I also want to thank my daughter, Kathy Feldheim, for her insights as a teacher and for the many conversations we had about this book. Many thanks also to Claudia Pitts and Carolyn Fabrick who shared their thoughts on bullying from the psychologist and the school psychologist point of view. For all the people that I don't have the space to name, please know that I acknowledge and appreciate all of your contributions.

A special thanks to Mary Lou Daugherty who lived with this book from conception through completion, offering ideas, rereading drafts, and always offering support and help. Also, thanks to Jessica Williams for all of her help compiling the booklist. Thanks to Susan Kovalik. Thanks to Irving Halperin and his wife Jill Kneeter for permission to use his bully narrative in this book. His death has left a hole in our lives. Finally, I want to thank all the children who participated in my research and whose words and writing are throughout this book. I admire your openness and courage and I hope that someday all schools will be a safe place for you.

Preface: Imagining a Better and Safer World Through Critical Literacy

Getting students to think about bullying and social justice through their reading and writing is part of a multicultural education. By doing so, we integrate and deepen students' literacy experiences and help them deal with bullies and/or imagine a better world.

I am not a psychologist or a counselor; I am a teacher who believes in the intellectual and transformative power of literacy to combat bullying in school. I love teaching. Before becoming a literacy professor, I spent eighteen years in elementary, middle, and high school classrooms—first grade, second grade, and K–12 writing workshops, especially with middle school students. Teaching is the central aspect of who I am and what I do. I look at everything in life as a learning opportunity, and the joy of learning has shaped my career.

I began teacher research in my own classroom in the early 1980s as I incorporated reading and writing workshops into my curriculum. Perhaps because I taught the first and second grades and was privileged to witness the miracle of children learning to read and write, my questions centered on literacy. How did some children come so naturally to reading and writing while others struggled? How could I support and facilitate the process? I noticed that when students were engaged in making meaning, their literacy skills developed and grew.

Over the years, my interest in literacy expanded to include older readers and writers. Most recently I've been working with middle school students. I am convinced that literacy is a tremendous vehicle for helping all students gain greater understanding and insight into the peoples of the globe. Literacy is a tool which opens up our world and helps us to better understand and accept all human beings.

Allan Luke and Peter Freebody (1999) discuss the social practices that human beings use to make meaning. Among these practices are reading texts as a code breaker, text participant, text user, or text analyst. Depending on these perspectives, you look at the text differently (Wilson 2002). For example, as a code breaker, you may concentrate on just reading the text. You might ask questions like, How do these letters and sounds go together? As a text participant, your questions focus on the meaning of the text: How do these ideas fit together? As a text user, you read pragmatically, figuring out what kind of text you're reading, how you will use it, and how others might use it. As a text analyst, you bring a critical perspective to the text asking questions like:

> Who wrote this?
> What's to gain?
> Is this true?
> What questions are asked?
> What questions aren't asked?
> Are all fathers, mothers, children, students, adults, and so on like this?
> Is this true for all members of this group?
> Might the character have responded in another way?
> What is the text trying to do to me?
> Whose interests are served by this text?
> Whose voice is silenced?

Although students may not always take a critical stance, this practice helps them critique the world and understand how texts contribute or don't contribute to making the world a more just and equitable place in which to live.

Hilary Janks (2001) believes that we must examine the link between language and power, especially "the way language is used to maintain and contest relations of domination" (p. 139). She sees critical literacy as deconstruction and then reconstruction. We need to see texts—those we agree with as well as those that are obviously a problem—from as many perspectives as possible. Once we understand the forces shaping ideas, we can reimagine and reconstruct a better world. According to Janks, we need human diversity to create new ideas. Critical literacy using multicultural children's literature is indeed central to creating democratic, fair, and hate-free schools that confront all forms of bullying and harassment.

How do we handle these difficult discussions in our classrooms? This book offers literacy practices and strategies that will build strong readers and writers who think about and are able to deal with bullying issues. By helping our students read about, write about, and discuss issues of consequence, we begin to make a difference.

A Note on Methodology

The data I collected for this book included field notes of my classroom observations, student manuscripts and written reflections, and transcriptions of audio- and videotapes of literature discussions and writing workshops. I also transcribed audiotapes of my interviews with teachers. To analyze these data, I followed the procedures set out by Matthew Miles and Michael Huberman in *Qualitative Data Analysis* (1994). Data collection and analysis occurred concurrently, as a recursive, interactive, and cyclical process.

An Adolescent's Tragedy

There he strolls down a lonely path.
He yearns for companionship but only feels their wrath.

Deep inside, a voice screams out.
Please let me be special, not always isolated with feelings of
    self-doubt.

The pain that he feels is oh so constant—it doesn't go away.
It opens the door and penetrates the emptiness as strongly as
    it did yesterday.

Please accept his differences and let him participate in your
    game.
It is only so tragic that the victim of the bully should feel
    such emotional strain.

—Jonathan Radke

Chapter One

Why a Book About Bullying?

[I learned that] most bullies have a reason they bully. That all people are different and they should be proud of themselves because they are different. That there are good and bad ways to express our anger. Some adults can't read and they need help. Homeless and hungry people can go to a soup kitchen where they get fed for free. That all people should be included in things no matter how they look. I also learned that there is a way I can help people and other children can too.

—Addie

What Is Bullying?

The April 25, 2001, issue of the *Journal of the American Medical Association* includes a large, quantitative study on bully behavior (Nansel, Overpeck, Pilla, Ruan, Simons-Morton, and Scheidt 2001). Bullying is described as a "specific type of aggression in which (1) the behavior is intended to harm or disturb, (2) the behavior occurs repeatedly over time, and (3) there is an imbalance of power, with a more powerful person or group attacking a less powerful one. This asymmetry of power may be physical or psychological, and the aggressive behavior may be verbal (e.g., name-calling, threats), physical (e.g., hitting), or psychological (e.g., rumors, shunning/exclusion)" (p. 2094). The study was based on a sample population of 15,686 students in grades 6 through 10.

Who Are the Victims?

The Nansel study cited above found that "males reported being bullied by being hit, slapped, or pushed more frequently than did females. Females more frequently reported being bullied through rumors or sexual comments" (p. 2097). Bullies and those bullied were lonelier and had poorer relationships with other students. Middle school boys indicated a positive correlation between bullying and being lonely. The study also found that bullying occurred "with greater frequency among middle school–aged youth than high school–aged youth" (p. 2098). (The researchers acknowledged that bullying in elementary schools wasn't looked at in this study and needed to be.)

Girls experience bullying somewhat differently than boys do. Although overt fighting among girls is increasing, this is still not the norm. Because society expects girls to "be nice," they're forced to hide their aggression and be subtler. Girls' "gossip" is often targeted to make one girl the outsider in an effort to build an affiliation among the other girls (Simmons 2002, p. 29). This is often done under the adult radar, so that the girl bully looks perfectly nice. Often, she never actually has to say the hurtful words to the victim: she gets one of the girls wanting to be linked to her popularity to help her. In her autobiography *Please Stop Laughing at Me* (2003), Jodee Blanco recalls the terror she felt about attending her high school reunion. She sat in her car for more than an hour, afraid to face the girl who had tormented her throughout high school. Although she was an accomplished journalist, her achievements faded away as she contemplated meeting her nemesis again.

Anyone who is "different" is susceptible to being bullied, but lesbian, gay, bisexual, and transgendered children and young people are among the most frequent victims. They are "seven times more likely than their peers to be threatened with or injured by a weapon in school and five times more likely to skip school because they do not feel safe" (Buckel

1999, p. 6). So are children in gay and lesbian families and students who are perceived to be gay or lesbian, whether they are or not.

When students are called names that include *gay* as a word of hate and their teachers do nothing, those students are not being protected. When children are taunted on the playground with pejoratives like *fag* or *homo*, *girly* (to boys), *sissy*, or *ugly*, etc. teachers often turn the other way. Though these teachers may believe they are working toward establishing safe and democratic classrooms, they are in reality doing the opposite. Although it is unintended, teachers who say and do nothing in such cases are letting children know that they and their families have no protection from the continuing assault of bigotry and prejudice.

This is not a religious issue but an equal rights issue. All children have the right to a safe and protected school environment. Regardless of how we as individuals may feel about homosexuality, as teachers and administrators it is our responsibility to be an advocate for every student in our classroom. We've seen the harm that bullying and harassment do to all children. We must step in and protect every one of them.

Jamie Nabozny was not protected in the Eau Claire, Wisconsin, public schools he attended. He appeared weak and effeminate and was picked on by his classmates. In middle school he was attacked and beaten up by some of the other boys. Initially, the principal brought in the bullies and their parents and Jamie and his parents to discuss the situation. But the beatings continued, and no further action was taken. Jamie's parents were told that they had to expect this sort of thing if their son was going to insist on being different.

The bullying continued in high school. Although Jamie went to the guidance counselor and the principal, nothing was done to stop the perpetrators. Horrible things were done to Jamie in the boy's bathroom. His head was held in the toilet, and the other boys mock raped him. Jamie dropped out of high school twice and finally ran away to Minneapolis. Several years later he sued the school district.

The nine jurors listened to damning testimony. Jamie had been subjected to name-calling, "hitting, kicking, being spat upon, punching, and things being thrown at him" (trial record, *Nabozny v. Podlesny*, p. 30). A letter written by a lawyer in Jamie's behalf recounted his abuse in middle school. It named the perpetuators and the administrator's response:

QUESTION: And isn't it true that the letter attributed to the principal the response, "Boys will be boys and that if Jamie wasn't so openly gay he wouldn't be having these problems in school?"

ANSWER: I believe so.

(*Nabozny v. Podlesny*, p. 33)

Jamie had been assaulted in a urinal and urinated on. He was also kicked in the stomach so severely that he required abdominal surgery.

The jurors decided that the Eau Claire schools had not protected Jamie. The school district itself was not found liable because they had safe-school language in their policies, but the principals and administrators who didn't protect Jamie were fined $900,000 dollars.

Other cases have followed. The Titusville, Pennsylvania, public schools paid $312,000 to gay student Timothy Dahle because the district did not protect him from physical and verbal abuse. The district settled with him in 2000, right before the case was to go to trial. Timothy too dropped out of school because he could no longer endure the harassment and abuse, which began for him in the sixth grade and included being hit and pushed down the stairs. He even attempted suicide (Weiss 2002). In Reno, Nevada, in 2002, Derek Henkle received a $451,000 settlement for the violence and harassment he received in his school district.

Studying discrimination as an aspect of civil rights provides the foundation for truly safe and inclusive classrooms. The equal protection clause in the Constitution requires the state to treat each person with equal regard, as having equal worth, regardless of his or her status: "We are unable to garner any rational basis for permitting one student to assault another based on the victim's sexual orientation" (from the decision in the Nabozny case). That's because there is none.

How Big a Problem Is It?

Pollack (1998) found that "the National Association of School Psychologists estimated that in the United States, some *160,000 children miss school every day for fear of being bullied*" (p. 343, italics mine). According to the *JAMA* study (Nansel, Overpeck, Pilla, Ruan, Simons-Morton, and Scheidt 2001), "A total of 29.9% of the sample reported moderate or frequent involvement in bullying, as a bully (13%), one who was bullied (10.6%), or both (6.3%)" (p. 2099). The study also found that former bullies are four times more likely to have a criminal record by the time they are twenty-four years old; that 60 percent of former bullies have at least one conviction and between 35 percent and 40 percent have three or more convictions; and that those who had been bullied had "higher levels of depression and poorer self-esteem at the age of twenty-three" (p. 2099).

Interestingly, another study contradicts the notion that bullies are unhappy. Svoboda (2004) discusses Juvonen's study of 2000 sixth graders in Los Angeles, which found the "bullies were consistently among the most liked and respected kids in school" (p. 20). The bullies had good self-esteem and were actually "privileged" by the rewards that came from bullying. As long as a crowd gathered to watch the bullies in action, the behavior continued. Juvonen believes that "teaching children not to applaud antagonizers by giving them attention can change social expectations and norms. Empowering them to intervene in bullying situations would be by far the most effective strategy" (p. 20).

All children are affected by bullying. Victims may be pursued on the basis of seeming different in any number of ways. They may be overweight or underweight, wear the wrong kind of clothes, or be a different color or religion. But the children who witness this harassment suffer as well. The posttraumatic stress that children experience as "either victims of or witnesses to violence includes intrusive imagery, emotional constriction or avoidance, fears of recurrence, sleep difficulties, disinterest in significant activities, and attention difficulties" (American Psychological Association 1993).

A Vicious Circle?

The truth behind the statistics is this: most bullies were bullied themselves. In Alice Miller's *For Your Own Good: Hidden Cruelty in Child-Rearing and the Roots of Violence* (1990), she examines Hitler's abusive childhood. His father was illegitimate and suffered throughout his lifetime because of it. (Even as a successful businessman in his forties, he still wanted to be legitimate, and his uncle finally adopted him.) In turn, Hitler's father was often physically abusive with his children and once nearly beat Hitler to death.

Miller postulates that when abused children grow up without a helping witness (more about this in a minute), they unleash their rage on others, often their own children. She writes, "Hitler never had a single other human being in whom he could confide his true feelings; he was not only mistreated but also prevented from experiencing and expressing his pain; he didn't have any children who could have served as objects for abreacting his hatred; and, finally, his lack of education did not allow him to ward off his hatred by intellectualizing it. Had a single one of these factors been different, perhaps he would never have become the arch-criminal he did" (p. xi).

But Hitler would not have been able to wreak so much havoc without the German population's willingness to go along. Miller also examined many child-rearing guides of Hitler's time. Book after book taught that the most important thing parents can teach their children is obedience. If a child wanted something, parents were urged not to give in, but instead to distract the child, so that the parent was always in control. This was also how teachers were expected to control their students. The German people had grown up with "all the components of a strict upbringing; the ruthless, dictatorial methods, the excessive supervision and control, the lack of understanding and empathy for the child's true needs" (p. 131). They were used to following orders.

Andrea Dworkin (2000) adds one more layer to thinking about how Hitler was able to kill so many people during the Holocaust. She shows that long before Hitler was born, there was fierce anti-Semitism in Germany and that Jews were regularly dehumanized through words. The old children's chant, "sticks and stones may break my bones, but names can never hurt me," doesn't get it right. Names hurt, and words are often a bully's first line of assault. Dworkin believes that without the hateful words, Hitler could not have gotten away with the killings. "The responsible were right to fear rhetoric as much as they feared marching men: words make killing easier, legitimate, or inevitable. Words can kill; and one cannot find killing without finding the words that accompany it" (p. 155). This happened to Matthew Shepard, in Laramie, Wyoming. First he was called names because he was a homosexual. Then he was beaten up, tied to a fence, and left to die.

Although Hitler and Matthew Shepard are extreme examples of the bully and the bullied, they remind us why it's important to stop bullying as early as possible.

What Can We Do About It?

We need to make a commitment to all our children. Clearly we need to confront bullying and harassment in our classrooms as they happen and provide opportunities to discuss preventative measures. The American Psychological Association recommends that remedial programs begin as early as possible so that they take advantage of developmental windows of opportunity when they are most needed or are most likely to make a difference (Sautter 1995).

The researchers who undertook the *JAMA* study theorize that "effective prevention will require a solid understanding of the social and environmental factors that facilitate and inhibit bullying and peer aggression. This knowledge could then be used to create school and social environments that promote healthy peer interactions and intolerance of bullying" (p. 2100). Their final recommendations include interventions to change "the school and classroom climate to increase awareness about bullying, increase teacher and parent involvement and supervision, form clear rules and strong social norms against bullying, and provide support and protection for individuals bullied" (p. 2100).

Alice Miller (2001) holds that one person can make a difference in the life of a child who is bullied and subjected to violence. She calls this person a helping or enlightened witness. She writes, "Children with no helping witness are in the greatest danger of regarding the dreadful things they have been subjected to as for their own good and then dealing out to others the same kind of treatment without the slightest pangs of conscience" (p. 62).

Miller goes on to explain that "denying and repressing our childhood traumas means reducing our capacity to think and conspiring to erect barriers in our minds" (p. 121). The enlightened witness is important because children learn that they are not crazy, that this abuse actually occurred, and that it is not their fault. "If someone is present to help us recognize [the abuse] we will no longer be forced to perpetuate those patterns blindly" (p. 97).

Miller thinks that the "the power for change" lies in a coalition of "enlightened parents and teachers committed to putting nonviolent education and parenting on a firm legislative footing" (p. 129). Richard Hazler (1996) would agree: "Conveying the moral commitment through your actions to fight injustice is more important than making the perfect response."

We have to teach students that negative words can hurt and are not ever acceptable in school.

How Can This Book Help?

The purpose of this book is to help children confront bullying and the accompanying harassment (by word or action) through critical literacy. When I began working on it, I had no idea where my journey would take me. I only knew that this topic is vital for our students, as important as any academic subject. It would be wonderful if children never experienced bullying and harassment, but even if we never discussed it, they would still encounter these issues. Children face teasing, bullying, and harassment every day in their school's hallways, lunchrooms, and playgrounds. To ignore it, as we have for so many years, allows this intolerable behavior to continue. Children need our strength and guidance to help them make ethical and caring decisions.

In my first book (Henkin 1998) I wrote about the inquiry cycle as a foundation for critical literacy. By starting with student questions, issues can be explored through inquiry, exploratory talk, literature and reading, media, interviews, writing, and reflection. The inclusive inquiry cycle (see Figure 1–1) is a framework for carefully examining issues of justice and fairness. It begins with all of our questions. It's a place where both teacher and students fight prejudice and discrimination to build a caring and collaborative community.

Meant to be inclusive, the cycle comprises but is not limited to all differently abled people, all religions, everyone in the class, all girls and boys, all races, reverence for the Earth, all families, all sexual identities, all economic classes, all ages, all historically oppressed people, and the workplace-oriented. I added the last category after working with teachers in Toronto. One high school teacher asked me to make sure that I included his students. "The students who are not on the college track are often treated as second-class citizens in their schools," he told me. Also, since September 11, teachers across North America have emphasized how Muslims and Arabs are now often treated unfairly and should receive special emphasis.

The ultimate point of inclusive inquiry is to teach for tolerance by creating hate-free zones in our classrooms. Another way to think about this is to imagine a house (see Figure 1–2; drawn by my student Connie Smyth, it shows all the specifics). Teaching for tolerance, fighting prejudice, and fighting for social justice therefore also become part of building democratic classrooms. And this social action is part of democratic and caring worlds. The full graphic then looks like the one in Figure 1–3.

Building on the inclusive inquiry cycle, students respond to texts through reading, writing, and discussion. It's not enough for children to talk about issues; we want them to do something positive. We need to encourage social action in the classroom, school, town or city, and world. I use the term *social justice* to

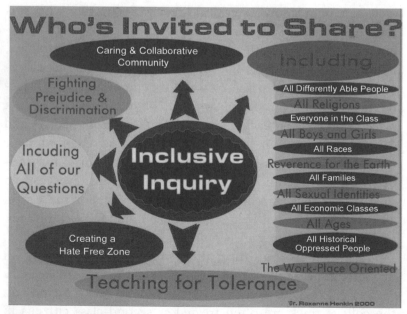

Figure 1–1.   The Inclusive Inquiry Cycle

express this idea. It's not enough for children to know that bullying, discrimination, and oppression are wrong; we must all work together to end them. How can children grow up to create a more democratic world if they haven't experienced democratic classrooms and democracy in their lives? I believe in the power of literacy to transform lives.

Reading and writing about issues like bullying lets students critique hateful words and use other words to fight bullying and harassment in all its forms. It makes sense to teach this, even when faced with the pressures of mandated testing. For students to achieve the greatest gains in reading and writing, they need lots of practice in a variety of genres. They need to read and write widely about content that is rich and meaningful. Reading and writing about issues related to bullying and harassment help students develop as ethical people as well as literate learners.

"Everyone must identify a personal role in the formal and informal policies that seek to reduce violence, harassment,

Figure 1–2.   Another View of the Inclusive Inquiry Cycle

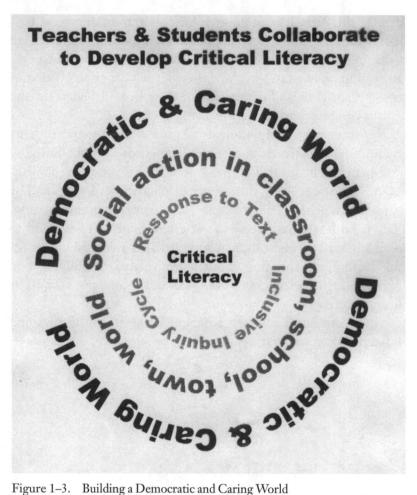

Figure 1–3.   Building a Democratic and Caring World

and bullying. . . . Only when individuals are aware of a problem can they begin to consider taking action" (Hazler 1996, p. 155). In confronting bullying and harassment through literacy, we bring an additional element into the conversation, one involving ethics and integrity. Robert Coles (1998) has said that if we want children capable of making ethical decisions, we need to bring up matters of conscience again and again (p. 9). By reading, writing, and thinking about bullying, we offer students "the thousands of ethical conversations" they need in order to grow into strong, literate adults.

This is a book about teaching reading and writing. As such, its primary focus is on developing comprehension skills. But as we're fostering students' literacy skills, we're using these skills to teach content. Students need to be reading and writing about something meaningful. It's my premise that the stories, themes, and lessons of history and modern life can be used to examine how people have dealt with bullying and harassment in productive ways. By combining the two, we create a rich literacy curriculum filled with opportunities for students to think through their decisions. Ultimately, we want students to be able to make good choices in school, on the playground, and at home.

But it can be difficult to talk about bullying when it involves specific students in our classroom. By looking at the ways other people deal with these issues, we help students develop a rich array of strategies to draw from when they are picked on. Good literature offers endless opportunities to think about and practice in our mind how we might act in similar situations. This book, then, is not about canned programs in either character education or reading. Instead, it offers rich strategies in which authentic character education emerges through reading and writing comprehension.

Chapter Two

One Model Classroom

I have learned many things. For one thing they hurt people because they have no friends. That's how bullies get attenchen. No one deserves to be bullied. I think it is mean. Bullies should try and be friends with other kids instead of being mean to everyone. But they don't know how.

—Nathan

*H*ow can we help students think about and deal with bullying? How can literacy support and deepen this work? I spent the 1999–2000 school year thinking about these questions while I was an observer in Ginger Weincek's third-grade classroom, in Elgin, Illinois. Ginger is an extraordinary teacher. She's innovative, sensitive, creative, and always eager to learn. Her classroom includes mixed races, cultures, and social classes. Ginger focuses on building classroom community, providing the language necessary to discuss the qualities that build character, and then highlighting those qualities in class discussions of literature and life. That year, Ginger, her students, and I faced the issues of bullying, anger, and prejudice together.

We found that concentrating solely on books about bullies wasn't effective. One reason for that can be derived from the work of Gerda Lerner (1997), who helps us understand that to fight one injustice, we need to fight them all. In fact, she says that we have had such limited success righting social wrongs because we haven't seen the large picture and worked on many fronts at the same time. Lerner cautions:

[a]s long as we regard class, race, and gender dominance as separate though overlapping systems, we fail to understand their actual integration. We also fail to see that they cannot be abolished se-

quentially, for like the many-headed hydra, they continually spawn new heads. . . . The system of hierarchies is interwoven, interpenetrating, interdependent. It is one system with a variety of aspects. Race, class, and gender oppression are inseparable; they construct, support, and reinforce one another. . . . The struggles against sexism, racism, anti-Semitism, and homophobia are inextricably linked (pp. 197–98).

Many of the books explicitly written about bullying are simplistic and not well written. They aren't as effective as multicultural and social issue books and books about history. Students know when something is simplistic or authentic and truthful. Rich literature that includes bullying as one among the many other complicated issues of living offers more to think about and discuss. Therefore, using criteria that Dr. Lorri Davis and I developed for social justice books, we compiled a list of well-written, captivating books that deal with wider issues. The criteria—used for both fiction and nonfiction—include:

- The book has been published relatively recently.
- The book is culturally authentic.
- The text and illustrations are accurately depicted, without stereotyping.
- The text and illustrations are detailed and vivid.
- The illustrations enhance the story.
- The book pushes or crosses the boundaries of diversity, depicting complex and complicated societal issues.
- The book raises important and/or controversial issues suitable for building character.
- The issues in the book are open to many interpretations, and different conclusions can be reached from them.
- The book stimulates questions.
- The book has the potential to prompt people to take social action.

The book list we developed, with annotations, can be found in Appendix B.

The students participated in small- and large-group literature discussions, creative dramatics, writing workshop, and reading workshop; listened to teacher read-alouds; and wrote their own reflections. I wanted to see how Coles' "thousands of ethical conversations" would play out in this classroom throughout the year, and I wanted to document the students' literacy growth.

The questions in my mind as I worked in Ginger's classroom were: What happens when students use literacy to think about social issues? What would their discussions look like? How would they talk about difficult ideas? Would their writing reflect their growing understanding of the concepts? I also wanted to discover how Ginger elicited and directed her students' ideas, discussions, and written responses.

Getting Started

Ginger begins each school year with an empty classroom and invites the students to set it up together. She assigns a planning group for each area. Students research, read, and write as they develop how their area will be set up and what it will contain. The plans are unique each year. For 1999–2000, the children created areas around the perimeter of the room, reserving the center for group activity. They set up a library containing books and plants, a listening center, a science center next to the sink, and many cozy nooks in which to sit and read.

Among Ginger's teaching techniques are giving many demonstrations—how to talk about books, how to participate in writing workshop—and offering her students many opportunities to reflect on their practice. She makes social justice personal. Her focus is on developing a caring community. "The key is allowing kids to talk and process their feelings. When you're trying to make a real difference in schools, it comes down to the kids—to their personalities—and the teachers, and what to do with the personalities that are threatened by growth. I think that it really is the personalities, and the desire to learn and grow. It all comes down to safety: how do you build a classroom where everyone feels safe?"

Her classroom is also about reflection. Ginger is a caring teacher who is open to change. It's not about how any particular day goes, it's about learning and growth. The goal is to become a lifelong learner. The students discuss issues that make a difference for them. They learn how to handle anger, fear, and uncertainty in their lives.

Finally, Ginger teaches for resiliency and social justice throughout the whole year. Every time she teaches a concept or demonstrates a reading strategy, she uses a social justice book. It doesn't happen just at the end of the year but through the work done day by day.

Teaching the Vocabulary

That year, Ginger's students began by learning the vocabulary of "lifeskills"—part of a curriculum for building character and community used in Susan Kovalik's Integrated Thematic Instruction model (Kovalik 2000)—and the textual-connection concepts discussed in *Mosaic of Thought* (Keene and Zimmerman 1997).

"Lifeskills" includes general lifelong guidelines and eighteen specific skills:

Lifelong Guidelines
- trustworththiness
- truthfulness
- active listening
- no put-downs
- personal best

Specific Lifeskills
- integrity: to act according to a sense of what's right and wrong
- initiative: to do something, of your own free will, because it needs to be done

- flexibility: to be willing to alter plans when necessary
- perseverance: to keep at it
- organization: to plan, arrange, and implement in an orderly way; to keep things orderly and ready to use
- sense of humor: to laugh and be playful without harming others
- effort: to do your best
- common sense: to use good judgment
- problem solving: to create solutions in difficult situations and to everyday problems
- responsibility: to respond when appropriate, to be accountable for your actions
- patience: to wait calmly for someone or something
- friendship: to make and keep a friend through mutual trust and caring
- curiosity: to investigate and seek understanding of your world
- cooperation: to work together toward a common goal
- caring: to feel and show concern for others
- courage: to act according to your beliefs
- pride: to achieve satisfaction from doing your personal best
- resourcefulness: to respond to challenges

First, Ginger and her students discussed each lifeskill, decided what it meant, and talked about how they might use it. Then as events occurred in the classroom or in the texts they were reading, students began pointing out the lifeskills when they encountered them. For example, when a text was difficult for him, Andrew said, "I'm using the lifeskill of perseverance to read this." The lifeskills became a natural part of the school day.

In the same way, Ginger incorporated *Mosaic of Thought's* ideas related to connections that can be made to texts. She introduced the vocabulary of *text-to-self*, *text-to-text*, and *text-to-world* by demonstrating the kinds of connections that she made to various kinds of texts as she read aloud, thinking out loud for the students' benefit. Then she invited students to try to make the same connections. Next, she had students note on the bulletin board the specific kinds of connections they made.

By October, the students were regularly incorporating both the lifeskills and *Mosaic of Thought* vocabulary.

Social justice themes were evident throughout the year. Topics dealt with included:

- teasing
- adult illiteracy
- anger
- homelessness and hunger
- gender issues
- bullying

Reading, literature discussions, and writing were always part of the work. Ginger facilitated student discussions, prompting students to think about issues as deeply as possible.

Investigating Anger

The book *Angry Arthur* (Oram 1997) is an excellent way to introduce the topic of anger, an emotion felt by both bullies and bystanders. What do you do with all the anger you feel inside? In the book, Arthur is so upset with his mother that he starts a storm. After the class read the book in February, the students had the following discussion.

GINGER: How many people have arguments with even their friends? So you work it out?

MARK: When I get mad I hit and kick. I don't like getting mad. Getting mad is like—like—like getting kidnapped. I really hate getting mad, but everyone gets mad sometimes. I have a connection to the book, *Angry Arthur*. When I get mad, it seems like a hurricane to me.

SANDY: I mentioned in my [piece of writing] that I don't like being mad either, so it's kinda like a text-to-text.

GINGER: How is it a text-to-text?

SANDY: Because we both kinda wrote the same thing.

GINGER: So you both don't like getting mad.

JESSICA: It was nice when you said that getting mad was sort of like getting kidnapped.

GINGER: Tell why it seemed nice to you.

JESSICA: Because it was a very good way to describe it.

TOM: When I get angry I think that it's a hurricane, too.

KATHY: I have a lot of connections. Sometimes I get angry at my sister. She doesn't listen to me. She always asks me questions like this one, "How do you use this pencil sharpener?" and I say, "Like this," and she doesn't use it like that. She always uses it another way and then I get angry about her. She always tells my mom if I did something to her. When she tells my mom I always get more angry. When I am angry, I always count.

GINGER: Does anyone have any response for Kathy?

PATTY: I like how you say when you get angry, you always count.

MARK: I get mad at my sister, too.

KATHY: My sister and me get mad like your sister and you do.

GINGER: I have a connection. When I get mad at my house, I count, too. Sometimes I feel like I should count to a thousand, because I'm so angry. But counting does seem to help me think before I say something that isn't nice, so I try to count to settle down first.

KATHY: I always get mad because my mom doesn't take me to places I want, and my birthday's coming and I'm going to get very mad, because maybe she's not going to make me a party, and I have some money, and she said when you get a lot of money, you'll buy the cake.

MARK: I get mad when my dog digs in the garbage and takes everything out and then my sister says I saw it there even though I was in the living room and I always have to clean it up.

TORI: I get mad when my dog always makes a mess when she eats, because then I have to clean it up.

GINGER: I want everybody to think of one time they remember getting really angry. Take a minute to think and be exact. Don't just say, "I was mad at my sister." What happened that you got mad about?

This key discussion demonstrates how the children learned to express thoughts that might otherwise have remained unarticulated. For Mark to be able to say that he felt like a hurricane was inside him was significant. It resonated with the other children, and it laid the groundwork for deeper connections in the future. Teachers often ask me how students can be so articulate. Remember, it doesn't occur in each and every literature discussion, but the day-to-day work makes such reflection possible.

In this discussion, the students used vocabulary related to both character building and reading strategies. Both Ginger and the students incorporated wait time. Exploratory talk was evident, particularly related to the idea of kidnapping and feeling like a hurricane. Ginger asked for further explanation and encouraged elaboration. She also asked for questions and responses and shared her own connections.

Investigating Homelessness

A few weeks later, the children read *Fly Away Home*, by Eve Bunting (1993). In this book, a homeless father and son are bullied by the security people at the airport, where they try to sleep and clean up. Here's what a group of students said in a "fishbowl" discussion that the rest of the class observed.

Kevin: I think his dad doesn't have a job. I feel sad for them.

Jeff: That's like my dad—he got a job, then he got fired. Then he went to another job. Then he got fired from that one. He worked for a place in the airport, and he worked for another job for buildings, and he was doing good so far, and then the boss said it didn't work out for him 'cause, uh, I don't know why, and then Jason offered me work for him, but my dad didn't like buildings—doing buildings—so he got fired.

Ginger: Jeff, can you tell us why you shared with us?

Jeff: The airport, because he was fired because he was late all the time.

Jason: Did your dad get fired because it was far away from the house?

Jeff: It was far away. He just couldn't get there in time.

Ginger: What connections do you think might be happening for Jeff? Just the middle people.

Ronald: Are you like—is your dad like the dad in the story because he's getting fired from his jobs and then he can't get too much money?

Jeff: Yeah, we only have a little house as our house now, because my mom is working right now, and because my dad doesn't have work he always picks me up.

Ginger: Can anyone else connect with what Jeff is talking about or with the story?

Howard: My dad got fired once because the boss was using the wrong kind of paint and he didn't want to wreck the people's apartment so he spoke up to the boss and then he got fired.

Jeff: Did your dad get a new job yet?

Howard: Yeah. He's, um, painting big buildings in Chicago.

John: Howard, did your dad, um, when he spoke up to the boss, the boss didn't like it, what he said?

Ginger: Is that why he got fired? 'Cause he spoke up to the boss? What did you guys think about that? Ronald, did you have something else?

Ronald: Why did your dad just, like—because he was telling the boss what he did wrong? Because if he didn't, he might have done it again and wrecked more apartments and then he could end up getting fired?

Howard: Yeah.

Ginger: What do you think about your dad doing that?

Howard: He did the right thing, because he didn't just, like, wreck all the apartments.

Jeff: When your dad still had the old job, did your dad give the boss the paints to use or did someone else?

Howard: No, the boss picked out the paint and the paint was like wrecking the houses.

Jeff: So why did he get fired?

Howard: Because he was telling the bosses that the paint didn't work and the boss really liked the paint, but my dad didn't, and he got fired.

Ronald: Um, a couple of years ago my dad was a carpenter and he still is but he got fired—fired from it—because he was new, and he was doing some things wrong, but he wasn't, like, working on what he was supposed to be doing; and a couple years later there was another new guy, who was, like, messing up on a lot of stuff, and then my dad got real mad at him and stuff, and then he was yelling at him about what he did wrong and stuff, and then he got fired.

Jeff: Ronald, I have two questions for you. Where does your dad work?

Ronald: He works—I think he works for contractors and, um, it's like the electric company, Con Ed.

Jeff: And do you know what was he doing wrong?

Ronald: He was, like, when he was building buildings with people, he wasn't putting the bricks in right, and then they were straight on top of each other and not like one right there, and one right there, and one right there, and so I think that was one of things he did wrong, and I forgot the others.

Jerry: Ronald, you know the new guy that you were talking about, what did he do wrong?

Ronald: Well, my mom told me this story a little while ago because my dad told her and she told me and—and he—but she didn't really tell me what he did wrong, just that he did something wrong.

This discussion was a turning point. It was authentic. Although Ginger prompted some responses, the boys in this group discussed the issues for long periods without her intervention. They were all interested participants, asking lots of questions. They used what they knew about their fathers' work experiences to deepen their understanding about why the father in the book might be out of work. They were talking animatedly, leaning forward, eager to hear every word and to contribute to the conversation. We observers were then able to go back and try to capture what we saw and explain why we thought it was a powerful discussion. Students began to internalize the concepts.

Putting It in Writing

In these kinds of discussions, students tackled critical issues. They were able to expand, elaborate on, and explore their ideas and carry them over into their reading, writing, and thinking in thoughtful, reflective ways.

Writing was particularly important to students' comprehension. Students wrote after reading or hearing texts, before discussing them. They often extended these initial writing responses during writing workshop. Writing was thus both the jumping-off point for and a summary of their discussions.

Investigating Bullying

In April we synthesized our work on bullying. Again, we spent most of the time with books that represented social justice issues in which the bullying theme was present but not exclusive. We wanted to help students become allies for victims, to be able to support fellow students.

These eight-year-olds shared many instances of bullying and teasing, some of which had occurred right before the discussion.

- "Today, this morning, when I walked in, I heard 'four eyes' but no one had glasses in this class. But Ashley just got glasses, and when I heard it I toled myself it's not true, it's not true." (Susan)
- "Some people make fun of my name and I say, 'I like my name so don't make fun of it.'" (Ian)
- "My cousin Hope Gay has an unusual last name, but I like it and so does Hope, but some of my friends think her last name is dumb and they think she's gay because of her last name." (Bianca)
- "My sister always calls me gay and I always tell her I'm not but she keeps telling me." (Annaliese)
- One of the children said she heard someone say *gay* during lunch recess.
- Many of the children reported that either they heard someone called *gay* or they themselves had been called the name.

Children were called names most often because of body weight (too much or too little) and for wearing glasses. In the beginning of the year, some of the students laughed when name-calling was discussed. As we worked throughout the year on some of these issues, the children's writing began to show empathy and more understanding. In April, Greg wrote:

> I think kids are bullyed because when they were Little they were bullyed. So thay are so use to it They fite back. And that lets the bully now he can Bully him some more.

As the discussions deepened, children role-played situations in which they could turn around potentially difficult situations. They also compiled a list of strategies for dealing with bullies:

1. Walk away from a bully.
2. Ignore the bully.
3. Tell someone like a teacher, parent, or friend who will help.
4. Try to be nice to a bully.
5. Try to be tricky.
6. Go to a class to talk about problems.
7. Stand behind the person being bullied.
8. Go out of your way to make new friends to make yourself feel better.
9. Tell the bully how it makes you feel.
10. Use humor. Tell a joke.
11. Stay with other people so you're not alone with the bully.
12. Don't give the bully power to change your life.
13. Don't fight back. It makes it worse.
14. Yell "No!" and get away.
15. Talk to a social worker.
16. Have an older person with you.
17. Talk to the school police officer.
18. Don't stand by and watch someone else being bullied. Use courage.

Even children who had bullied other students gained insight about why they did it. Robert wrote:

> When I was being mean I felt like this was worthless. But I keped on doing it. I was hart inside. I wanted someone else to get hurt like me. But I was hurting someone. I felt very bad. I did not want to hurt my friend. I was not happy I did not want to be happy. I felt like this was good and I did not want to be happy. I felt like this was good and I also felt this was very very mean. I felt bad.

What It All Comes Down To

The complexity of Ginger's literacy program contributed to the students' academic and social growth during the year. The interconnectedness of both text and language was present every day and wove the community together. Ginger continued to share social justice books, every day of the year. Students knew the value of their shared experience.

Chapter Three

Creating a Classroom That Focuses on Key Literacy Strategies

Some parents do not talk to their children about these topics. I think it is good we took the time to study these things at school because then we have more friends and a better place to live. I think learning about these things helped me because I told my sister about it so at school she is nice and we get along better.

—Addie

*B*ut how can I make my classroom like Ginger's? you may be asking. How do I get students to talk about books? How do I get them to write about meaningful topics? And it's true that teachers are often up against it. Take this response, written by a third grader after his teacher had read aloud *Your Move*, by Eve Bunting (1998), and one typical of both the discussions the children in this class had and the writing they did after they had either heard a picture book read aloud or read it by themselves:

> When I heard the story of the [book] *Your Move*. It was sad because he got hout [hurt], and it wa[s] happy because he didit want the hat and he didit gine [join] the club.

After saying a book was sad or happy, good or bad, these students were at a loss for words.

Good discussions focus on comprehension. How do these high-level discussions come about? What can teachers do to facilitate them? Even though there are many books about literature discussions, book clubs, and literature circles, this is probably the area about which teachers have the most questions. What exactly are they supposed to do? What are the students supposed to do? How will they know their discussions are of high quality?

Karen Smith (1995) recommends starting with a short text. She uses picture books, even with middle schoolers, because they are brief and students get to the discussion quickly. I've used her suggestions many times when demonstrating discussion with my students. I talk about how discussions are like gardens. First, we plant the seeds of our ideas. Next, we watch them grow into a tree. Then, we add branches and the tree blooms.

Let's look at some reading strategies that help students develop their reading comprehension skills and that work well with an antibullying, safe-schools curriculum.

The Directed Reading-Thinking Activity

This strategy is an excellent way to begin to develop comprehension. Before using a book, read the text carefully yourself and decide on one or two stopping points. This is very important. You want to find the points that will generate the most discussion. One mistake teachers often make is stopping too often or stopping when the answer is readily apparent. Instead, choose significant points in the text where the answer is not self-evident or is open to more than one interpretation.

Next read the story aloud (or have the students read it to themselves) up to the first stopping point. Then close the book and ask, "What do you think will happen?" Sometimes students will give reasons with their predictions. If they don't, you can ask, "Why do you think so?" Next, read the text to the second stopping point and ask for predictions again.

This procedure is deceptively simple. Teachers often feel that it is their job to probe, asking many questions that will help their students comprehend. This is counterproductive. It is during the students' discussion of their predictions that learning occurs. Therefore, it's important to keep quiet, thereby encouraging students to discuss the issues among themselves.

Likewise, when you try to encourage students by praising them, you're creating a situation in which yours is the right answer and the students are trying to guess it. Courtney Cazden, in her groundbreaking book *Classroom Discourse: The Language of Teaching and Learning* (1988), says that in many classrooms, discussion follows the typical initiation, response, evaluation sequence: the teacher initiates the question, the child responds, and then the teacher evaluates the student's response.

A directed reading-thinking activity (DR-TA) is designed to facilitate much more discussion among all students without the teacher constantly evaluating every response. There is no correct answer. Even if students predict outcomes that are different from the one in the text, these can be feasible and may even be better than the one the author uses. With a DR-TA, you're trying to brainstorm as many answers as possible rather than find just one correct answer.

Another mistake teachers often make with DR-TA is to have students write their predictions. Although this may occasionally be beneficial as a variation, your purpose is to promote discussion, and the time spent writing is time *not spent* talking. Your focus should be on rich discussion through prediction.

Small Groups

If you find that initially students aren't offering many predictions, you may want to have students first talk together in small groups. Small-group discussions allow more students to be heard, but they need to be thought through carefully. Students need to feel safe enough to venture their opinions and need to be taught the skills that allow everyone a chance to speak.

The first issue is group makeup and size. There are many books on group dynamics that include suggestions about how to group students. If you allow students to choose their own group, you're creating a situation of insiders and outsiders; the students who are not chosen or are chosen last are left feeling very vulnerable. Some form of random selection, like picking names out of a bag or counting off by numbers, is best. Also, it's important that the groups include both girls and boys.

Once in a group, each student needs to have an equal chance to speak. We need to teach students how to honor all students' voices. I ask students to make sure that they are facing each other.

One strategy you might choose to encourage equal participation is to ask each member of the small group to "say something" (Short, Harste, and Burke 1996) in response to the story. This can be anything, perhaps how she feels about the story, what he noticed, or comments about the characters. Then have the students go around again, this time either making predictions about the text or commenting on someone else's predictions.

I invite students who know they are shy and tend not to speak to push themselves to participate more. By the same token, I invite students who know they tend to talk a lot to step back after they've shared so others can have a chance. I also ask that each time the group meets, a different person is allowed to go first. Often, the first speaker gets more time and the last person who shares is hurried. By alternating, everyone gets a chance to go first at some point.

Demonstrations

One of the books I use with early demonstrations is *Cheyenne, Again,* by Eve Bunting. In this book, the main character is taken away from his family and brought to an Indian school. He is made to feel ashamed of himself, and he tries to run away. He is bullied over and over again by the adults at the school. Finally, he encounters a teacher who encourages him to stay strong and be proud of himself.

After reading the book, I ask students what their questions are. Younger students share their questions aloud. Older students write down their questions first, and I then ask for volunteers to share what they have written. (This ensures that everyone is prepared to respond orally, though they can still elect not to. To ensure rich discussion we don't introduce writing until after the reading of the book is completed.) I point out that each time they ask a question, they are planting the seeds of an idea. Some of the questions students may have in relation to this book are:

- Why was he taken away from his family?
- Why was he put in the Indian school?
- Why were the teachers so mean?
- Why was he bullied?
- What were the teachers scared of?

Next, I demonstrate how they can make their ideas grow. We choose one question with which to model our discussion. One discussion of "Why was he taken away from his family?" went like this:

"They didn't want them to be Indians."
"They didn't want them to see their moms and dads."
"They were mean people."
"They didn't know any better."

I tell students this is what I want them to do in their small-group discussions, too.

Finally, I point out that in order to have rich literature discussions, they need to listen carefully to what the speaker is saying and respond in thoughtful ways. They're not just trying to come up with lots of ideas but to build on questions and ideas that other students have posed. This is what happened in the following interchange, in which students discussed why the authorities have taken the main character away from his family.

HARRY: They thought they were doing the right thing.

MELISSA: But how could they have thought that? It doesn't make sense.

JOAN: Well, it was the law.

JAKE: But it was a bad law.

JESSIE: Sometimes laws are meant to be broken.

JAKE: What do you mean?

JESSIE: Like Rosa Parks. There are bad laws that you have to stand up to.

At the end of the demonstration, I praise the students and talk about all the things they've done well. They've listened to each other, posed questions, and thought deeply about the text together. They've made branches on the tree. They've had a rich literature discussion.

My follow-up demonstration also begins with a picture book. This time, after the text is read, students write down their questions and then form small groups. They take turns, first sharing their questions, and then making their questions grow.

Discussion Chains

This is a very concrete way to get students to see how discussion works. First, have a number of strips of paper ready. After reading the text, as the children in the class share their questions, write each question on a strip of paper in a different-color ink. Then take one question and have the students discuss it. Also write each statement they make about this question on a strip of paper. Use a different-color ink than the one the question is written in, and number the slips in the order the statements are made. The students can then make a "discussion chain," starting with the question, followed by all the statements that were made about it.

For example, the above discussion of *Cheyenne Again* would look like this:

> Strip of paper in red ink: Why did they take him away from his family?
> Strip 1 in pink ink (Harry): They thought they were doing the right thing.
> Strip 2 in pink ink (Melissa): But how could they have thought that?
> Strip 3 in pink ink (Melissa): It doesn't make sense.
> Strip 4 in pink ink (Joan): Well, it was the law.

Strip 5 in pink ink (Jake): But it was a bad law.

Strip 6 in pink ink (Jessie): Sometimes laws are meant to be broken.

Strip 7 in pink ink (Jake): What do you mean?

Strip 8 in pink ink (Jessie): Like Rosa Parks. There are bad laws that you have to stand up to.

When all these strips are interlinked in order and hung up in the classroom, the students have a concrete visual image of their discussion.

Similarly, Karen Spear, in her book *Sharing Writing* (1988), suggests that older students can be asked to chart a class discussion while it is happening, so that they are able to review the main points and issues they have raised. She also has students watch debates on public television and contrast them with interviews by someone like Barbara Walters, being on the lookout for real listening and give-and-take during the discussion.

Reader Response

When my colleague Lorri Davis and I facilitate literature discussions, we honor Louise Rosenblatt's reader-response theory. We use the following steps:

1. Read the book aloud.
2. Have each student write an individual response.
3. Let students share these responses in a small group.
4. Ask students to select another book (something no one is familiar with). Being able to choose the text conveys power.
5. Read the chosen text aloud, giving students the opportunity to really study the pictures.
6. Let students share their responses in small groups. (Everyone should feel safe enough to be comfortable sharing his or her biases.)
7. Move on to a whole-class share, in which the students get a chance to examine their beliefs and assumptions,

make connections to their personal experiences, and begin to analyze their and their classmates' reactions.

8. Talk about the process.

Some Final Points

Reading books is a very powerful way to initiate discussions, and these discussions should last for thirty to forty-five minutes. Students need a substantial chunk of time in which to develop their skill as facilitators, unfold their ideas, and refine their role as active listeners. Exploratory talk should be encouraged. Intertextuality (two texts, a text and a video, text and artwork) and/or multiple literacies can be crucial to widening the experiences and beliefs that students share, encouraging them to articulate hard-to-get-at beliefs and assumptions and reveal what they truly believe. Once students make personal connections with books, they reexamine and extend prior experiences and beliefs.

Robert Coles (1998) suggests that we nourish our moral imagination, "that 'place' in our heads, our thinking and daydreaming, our wandering and worrying lives, where we try to decide what we ought or ought not to do, and why, and how we ought to get on with people" (p. 7). We need to start educating students about these issues much sooner, while children are young. Literacy is a vehicle whereby children can begin to think about these issues before they escalate out of control.

Reflection is key, and video- or audiotaped student discussions are excellent impetuses. Giving students ample opportunities to think about and talk about their discussions helps their discussions improve. By pointing out what students do well, we develop students who can discuss text better and more fluently. When we ask students to apply this ability to high-quality books about social issues, we help them think about unfair situations like bullying and harassment and come up with strategies for responding to these situations.

Chapter Four

Sample Lessons

Do you think handicapped people should be included in all things? You might not think so, but I do. Just because they have disabilities doesn't mean that they can't do what others can. They can play sports, games, musical instruments, and do everything anyone else can. A person in a wheelchair could probably beat me in a game of basketball. My Godfather's brother has Downs Syndrome. He cuts the grass for his parents every week. I can't even start a lawnmower. People with disabilities are just as good as everyone else.

—Dean Stout, *Everyone Is Included*

The following lesson plans offer ideas on how to help students confront bullying through literacy. These are sample lessons that are meant to be flexible. Take what is useful and change the plans as needed depending on your students and the texts you are using.

Sample Lesson 1
Text: *Making Up Megaboy.*
Author: Virginia Walter.
Illustrator: Katrina Roeckelein.
Summary: The story of a thirteen-year-old boy who shoots a Korean liquor store owner, as filtered through eighteen brief first-person perspectives.
Grade level: 5–8.
Issues: Korean store owners are bullied by neighborhood children.
Reading strategies: Read-aloud or have students read the text silently.
Writing strategies: Stop and write, writing workshop.

Lesson Plan

- Either read the text aloud or have students read silently. After reading four of the eyewitnesses' perspectives, have the students stop and write their perceptions.
- Continue either the read-aloud or the silent reading for another four eyewitnesses' perspectives. Then students will again stop and write their ideas, thoughts, and feelings. The stop and writes shouldn't take longer than five minutes.
- Finish reading the book or have the students finish reading it.
- Have the students write a final response to the book. Again, this should be brief.
- In small groups of three or four, have the students share their writing. Then ask them to continue discussing their ideas about the book together.
- Use questions from the Bully Worksheet (Appendix A). Who were the bullies? Who was bullied? Why?
- Critical literacy questions: Whose point of view was represented? This is an excellent book for point of view. Because so many different points of view are offered, critically examining each can lead to discussions of perspective, point of view, and how the story was affected by them.
- Classroom insights: When Mickey Nuccio, a teacher at the Jose de Diego school in Chicago, used this book with students in her classes, she was shocked to discover that they did not empathize with the Korean store owner who was shot and felt his widow should go back to her own country. They also focused on Robbie's clothes, saying that they would never wear clothes from K-Mart or other discount stores. Mickey realized that she needed to continue this work, gently guiding the students to think about ethical issues.

Sample Lesson 2

Text: *Cheyenne Again.*
Author: Eve Bunting.
Illustrator: Irving Toddy.

Summary: The main character is taken away from his family and brought to an Indian school. He is made to feel ashamed of himself, and he tries to run away. He is bullied over and over again by the adults at the school.

Grade level: 2–6.

Issues: Young Bull is taken from his family and told to become a white man. His home, food, language, clothing, and beliefs are all taken from him. He is bullied by the system and the school.

Reading strategies: Read-aloud, directed reading-thinking activity (DR-TA), text-to-self, text-to-text, text-to-world, critical literacy.

Writing strategies: Stop and write, writing workshop, sketch to stretch.

Lesson Plan

- Read the text aloud to the class.
- Do a DR-TA. Stop at page 11, where Young Bull is looking at the room with all the empty beds. Ask students, "What do you think will happen?" and "Why do you think so?"
- Have students share their responses. When they have finished, continue reading.
- Read until page 23, where the boy is out in the blizzard. Ask again, "What do you think will happen?" and "Why do you think so?"
- Students again share their responses in the whole group.
- Ask students to turn to a partner and share their text-to-self responses such as "This book made me feel or think about . . ."
- Have students share their text-to-text responses such as "This book reminds of _____ book because . . ."
- Students can then share their text-to-world responses. "This book is just like what is happening in the news because . . ."
- Have the students stop and write what they are thinking about.

- Students then share their ideas in small groups.
- Next have them fill out the Bully Worksheet (Appendix A).
- Students then could do "sketch to stretch," (Short, Harste, and Burke 1996). Ask them to draw the pictures and feelings that they now have after reading the book. They can sketch what the story means to them. Reassure them that there is no correct way to draw and that they can be as abstract and creative as they like.
- In small groups, share each sketch. The other group members try to interpret the drawing. After every one has had a chance to share, students choose one sketch to share in the large group.
- Conclude with large group sharing of sketches.

Classroom Insights

After Mickey Nuccio read the book to her students, one student wrote:

> He was bothered when they told him he should forget all about his race and were he's from. I think that no one should be bulied about there race or were the came from No one should be told to forget about there race. I think it's unfair. People have talked about my race. But it doesn't really bother me because no one can make me feel any differently about my race because I'm proud of being Poerto Rican. An no one could ever make me change my mind about who I am were I from or what I believe in that's what I think.

Another student wrote:

> Bullying was when Cheyenne was trying to run away from the school and some guy caught him and put him and some guy forced him to wear uniforms and, wearing boots that were uncomfortable.
>
> The bullying was not that bad because there must be disciplining for running away from school.
>
> I have been bullied lots of times By people talking about my mom. I't getting threatened. I've seen kids and my friends get bullied a lot they've even got beat up.

If I were to see kids get bullied by older kids I would try to get help or to try to help them. Sometimes I would try to tell them off.

Both students had strong feelings and were able to share their beliefs clearly.

Sample Lesson 3

Text: *It Doesn't Have to Be This Way: A Barrio Story.*

Author: Luis J. Rodriguez (a former gang member).

Illustrator: Daniel Galvez.

Summary: Moncho is considering joining a gang whose members bully each other as well as innocent victims. His cousin Dreamer is accidentally shot when she tries to talk Moncho out of joining the gang.

Grade level: 4–8.

Issues: Gang violence.

Reading strategies: Silent reading or read-aloud, DR-TA.

Writing strategies: Stop and write, writing workshop.

Lesson Plan

- If the students are silently reading copies of the text, tell them to read to page 10 and then close the book. If you're reading aloud, do the same. Read until page 10.
- In small groups, have students discuss, "What do you think will happen?" and "Why do you think so?"
- Some of the students can share their ideas in the large group.
- Students can continue reading, or you can continue the read-aloud until page 22.
- Again, have them answer the questions, "What do you think will happen?" and "Why do you think so?" in small groups.
- After they've finished, have the students do a stop and write.
- Then have the students fill out a Bully Worksheet (Appendix A).
- Move into writing workshop. Give students the option to continue their stop and writes or they can write bully nar-

ratives about a time they were either bullied, were a witness to bullying, or bullied someone.

- At the end of writing workshop, students gather with their stop and writes, Bully Worksheets, bully narratives, and other manuscripts. In small groups, students can share from any of these. Have students follow this with a discussion of what they've learned and what they are thinking about bullying.
- Bring students back to the large group and finish the discussion.

Classroom Insights

After reading the story, one of Mickey Nuccio's students wrote:

> I think that Dreamer was more responsible than Moncho, because she cared for him and since she cared so much for him she got shot. Whats going to happen next is Moncho is going to notice how much she cares so now he is going to do all he can just to make her happy. And since Dreamer got shot, I think she is still going to survive.

> Comments:
> Maybe Moncho should get out the gang if he cares so much for Dreamer. Dreamer shouldn't care so much for her cousin, because if he doesn't care much about her that's why he's in a gang.

> Questions:
> Does Moncho really want to be in that gang?

This student is starting to examine the ethical issues involved in Moncho's decision.

Sample Lesson 4
  Text: *Who Belongs Here? An American Story.*
  Author: Margy Burns Knight.
  Illustrator: Anne Sibley O'Brien.
  Summary: This beautifully written story is told using two
    genres. Based on a true story, the fictional tale centers

on Nary, a boy from Cambodia who has moved to the United States from a refugee camp in Thailand. Nary is amazed by life in the United States but puzzled by the reaction of some classmates who tell him to go back to where he belongs. (The compelling illustration here is a picture of an empty hallway with open lockers; the text below the picture asks what would happen if everyone in the United States who originally came from somewhere else was asked to leave.) Simultaneous nonfiction text provides facts about each of the topics raised in the text: immigration, languages spoken in the United States, U.S. food origins, and so on.

Grade level: 3–6.

Issues: Students bullying Nary; refugees fleeing their home country.

Reading strategies: Read-aloud, DR-TA, text-to-self, text-to-text, text-to-world, critical literacy.

Writing strategies: writing response, writing workshop, poetry.

Lesson Plan

- Read the text aloud to the class.
- Do a DR-TA. Stop at the page with the empty lockers. Ask students, "What would happen if all the people in the United States whose family came from some other country were asked to go back to where they came from?" Have the students divide into small groups and discuss this question.
- After a few minutes, have the class come back together and share their responses.
- Continue reading the book until the end.
- Ask children to write a response to the text. How are they feeling now? What stands out in the story? What questions do they have? What are they wondering about?
- Ask the class to return to their small groups and share their responses to the story.

- Suggested questions from the Bully Worksheet to generate discussion: Where did bullying come into the story? Who was bullied? Why? Who were the bullies? Who stood up to the bullies (who were Nary's allies)? Who were the innocent bystanders? What actions were taken to deal with the bullies? Were they effective? What other actions could have been taken? Who else could have helped Nary? What other themes of bullying were in the text? The whole reason Nary was in the United States was because his country was overthrown by another. In what way are refugees bullied? How has Nary's family attempted to help him deal with the bullying and violence in his life? What connections can you make to other texts, to yourself, and to the world?
- Critical literacy questions: Whose point of view was represented? Whose point of view was not represented? What other points of view could a person have? What was the author trying to get across? What would have happened if Nary hadn't been bullied by the students? How would that have changed the outcome of the story? What if Nary had reacted by fighting back? How would that have changed the story?
- Have students write a "Where I'm From" poem (Christensen 2000). The original "Where I'm From" poem was written by Kentucky author George Ella Lyon. The poem can structured in a variety of ways. Leah Miller and Elsa Statzner, from National-Louis University, in Chicago, suggest the following:

> In the first two lines, write *I am from* and then list foods that are special to your family. In the next two lines list holidays or experiences that are special to your family. In the second stanza concentrate on specific locations in your house. In the third stanza describe important people in your life and familiar sayings or beliefs. In the fourth stanza, talk about your culture and where you are from.

While having the class write, write your own poem and share it with the students.

Where I'm From

by *Roxanne Henkin*

I am from lox and bagels, fried matzah,
Chicken soup, kugel, and borscht,
at Passover and Rosh Hashanah in my
Grandparents' dining rooms.

I am from long tables that fill the dining room,
Where there is always room for one more.
I am from my Bubby and Grandmother,
And Grandfather whose smiling faces have vanished from
   the earth.

I am from Skokie, from "Knock on wood"
and "Wear it in good health."
I am from "No one cares for you like your family" and
"Be wary, the Holocaust was just yesterday."

I am from the Jewish people,
Persecuted through the past millenniums,
The Holocaust taught to my ten-year-old self,
Forever haunting our happy lives.

Chapter Five

Writing About Bullying

People walk away when I talk
    I am only a child of eleven
But I have views on heaven!
    I am the future of the
nation. I am inspiration!
    I am free, leave me be!
Please just listen to me!
    I am strong! Maybe
My views are wrong.
    I am power not a "coward,"
    just listen to me!
How I hate and despise when
People won't sympathize.
    I am the key to the nation.
Do I have to draw an
Illustration?
Just listen to me.
        —Tyler, *Listen to Me*

Writing Workshop

The premise of this book is simple: use the best literacy strategies you have at your disposal to confront the issues of bullying and harassment in your classroom. In the case of writing, best practice means writing workshop (Atwell 1998; Graves 1994; Zemelman and Daniels 1988). Typically, a writing workshop lasts between forty and fifty minutes and goes something like this:

- minilesson (five minutes)
- status of the class (optional; five minutes)

- writing and conferring (thirty minutes)
- sharing (ten minutes)

The minilesson is meant to be just that, a short lesson lasting no more than five minutes. Generally, you teach your students about some aspect of their writing that needs help based on your evaluation of their papers. (This doesn't mean that you never teach longer lessons about aspects of writing. It just means that you don't do so during writing workshop.)

Status of the class is a record-keeping system that allows you to keep track of what your students are writing and at what stage they are in the process. Many teachers prepare a chart with the days of the week on the vertical axis and the names of their students on the horizontal axis. Then they enter each student's topic and writing process stage on the grid each day.

During the major portion of the workshop students, individually and in pairs, write, revise, confer, edit, and publish their writing.

Finally a few students read their finished pieces or their works in progress.

Once students have internalized the process, a writing workshop proceeds more efficiently and can therefore be accomplished in a more condensed timeframe, perhaps something like this:

- minilesson (five minutes)
- writing and sharing (twenty minutes, during which you take the status of the class)

Following this model, students share and confer at will after five minutes of sustained silent writing. Whole-group sharing is optional and, if done, perhaps takes place once or twice a week. Peer conferences, in which student thinking is honored as ideas are shared, discussed, and expanded, are part of the process.

Getting the Juices Flowing

I often begin a writing workshop by asking students to write down, quickly, five things they might write about. I write my own list on the board a bit more slowly to make sure that everyone has time to record at least one idea before I bring them back together. I try to list ideas that demonstrate the range and depth of topics that students might choose, silly incidents as well as more serious topics. I usually start with pets, because so many children have their own pets and love to tell stories about them. A typical list might look like this:

Ellie (my dog) [or whatever; be specific]
Jessica (my other dog)
Emma (my cat)
Sasha (my nephew)
Central Park in Skokie, where I was bullied when I grew up

Even when I'm directly focusing on bullying, I still provide a range of topics and allow students to write about other things.

Then I point out that just because I've come up with these ideas, it doesn't necessarily mean I will end up writing about one of them. I need to talk my ideas through, discover what it is I want to say about them, decide whether I will be able to engage my audience. I relate some adventure Ellie, Jessica, and/or Emma and I have had. Then I share a story about an important decision Sasha's had to make while growing up. Finally, I focus on the fifth topic, the one that involves bullying.

"Central Park was one of the parks close to my home in Skokie, where I grew up. Skokie was about 40 percent Jewish then. I was playing at the park when a boy on a bicycle began chasing me. 'Jesus killer, Jesus killer,' he yelled. I ran away from him as fast as I could. I remember my heart pounding rapidly. I was both terrified and embarrassed. I was being bullied and I was being threatened." As soon as I began talking about this, I knew I needed to write about it.

Some teachers shy away from topics that can be emotional and/or controversial. Yet we know that good writing comes from the personal voice, and if we want students to think deeply about issues, they need to be real. We need to create safe writing classrooms in which students' voices can be heard.

Using Narratives

Narratives are compelling teaching tools in the classroom. We use stories to make sense of our lives (Davis, Sumara, and Luce-Kapler 2000, pp. 45–47). By writing and sharing narratives, we explore our identities and learn what we know and what we still need to learn. You can discuss the narratives below with your students in preparation for their writing narratives of their own.

This first narrative is by Irving Halperin (1999). When he was a child, in Chicago, his family—his parents and a brother—were very poor. His father bullied him and called him names but came through for his son in the incident Halperin describes.

> The new boy said to me on his first day in our grade school class, "I'll meet you after school." Without looking at me, that's all he said. At the time we were in the school yard during a recess. Other guys standing near us had heard him, so the word quickly spread that after school there was going to be a fight. Even as he issued his challenge, I knew that it had been a mistake to have hassled him. What if it turned out that he was good with his fists? I myself had never been in a fistfight. If he whipped me badly, the guys in my class would never let me forget it. After all, I had the advantage of being much taller and having much longer arms.
>
> From the beginning of his appearance in class, I had him tagged as a rube. His gym shoes were of an antiquated kind that only a hick wouldn't be embarrassed to wear. His shirt and trousers looked as though he had dressed for a formal event. So I was not surprised on overhearing him tell the teacher that he was from a small town in southern Illinois. I saw him as a prime target for ridicule.

He sat directly across the aisle from me, fixed like stone on his seat, apparently attentive to our English teacher. What prompted him to challenge me to a fistfight is that I had deliberately provoked him by continually interrupting his note-taking, asking to borrow his pencil, pretending that mine had been misplaced. My father's perennial victim, I became the harasser. What fueled my appetite for the game is that a student who had been observing my ploy reacted with audible amusement.

As the end of the school day drew near, my anxiety escalated. Momentarily, I considered ducking out and going straight home. But then he and the guys in the class would call me yellow, and I would never be able to live that down. So I had to fight.

When the bell ending the class rang, I moved slowly out of the building into the school yard. The new guy strode directly behind me, as though to block any attempt I might make to take off. A number of the would-be spectators went before us, as though they had taken it upon themselves to find a fight site. Their faces were flushed with the expectation of seeing blood drawn. I prayed that a teacher would come by and separate us before the fight could get underway.

In a far corner of the yard that was not visible from the school building's windows, the spectators formed a circle around the two of us. I glanced at my opponent. His eyes were steely, unwavering.

He immediately moved toward me. Wanting the onlookers to see that this did not intimidate me, I took a couple of steps toward him. We stood face to face. "Okay, wise guy," he said, his mouth tightly clenched. "You had your fun in class. Let's see what you can do now." He cocked his arms, as I had seen professional boxers do. That left no room for negotiation. So I cocked my right arm—my left was by far the weaker one. "C'mon, hook nose. Hit me," he challenged. Stung by his taunt, I desperately, wildly threw a roundhouse right at his head. With blinding speed, he blocked my hand as though brushing off a fly, and almost in the same instant his fist exploded against my nose. That punch had been executed in a compact, measured movement.

My face was on fire, blood gushed from my nose. The spectators were shouting, hooting; they wanted further action. Poker-faced, his gimletlike eyes were trained on me and his arms remained cocked. "What's the matter, big shot? You don't want to fight?" It was clear to me that if I dared to hit back there would be more than just a nose bleed—some teeth could be knocked out. I didn't answer. "You quit?" I nodded.

The one-punch fight was over. The spectators surrounded the victor, pumping his back, shoulders. Perhaps they already sensed that he would soon establish himself as one of the school's best fighters. Yet their adulation did not appear to please him; his poker-faced expression remained unchanged. Ignored, I remained apart from the others. My nose was covered with a blood-soaked handkerchief.

I hurriedly left the yard for home.

Shortly after that incident, I discovered that the new guy lived on our block. Our paths frequently crossed. Seeing him approach along the sidewalk, I would look away, to avoid giving him a pretext for a confrontation, and move over to the furthermost edge of the sidewalk. But this did not deter him from being provocative. "Hey, champ, let's mix it up for a couple rounds? Hey, Izzy, how's the schnoz doing?" And then he would deliberately shove me out of his way.

One afternoon after school, probably because I hadn't responded to his previous provocations, he slammed into me with such force that I went sprawling face down against the sidewalk. He stood above me, gloating. Blood dripped from my lips. "Next time watch where you walk, schnoz."

After he moved on, I rose and went to our apartment building. From the doorway, I glanced back over my shoulder. He was down the block, looking in my direction and making obscene gestures.

On entering our apartment, I intended to go directly to the bathroom and staunch the bleeding before my mother—this was the one day of the week that ordinarily she did not work in the store—could see me and make a big fuss. But she happened to be in the foyer when I entered and reacting to the sight of the blood-soaked handkerchief pressed against my lips, she cried out hysterically in Yiddish, "My God, what have you done to yourself!" I hurried past her to avoid an explanation.

When many minutes later I emerged from the bathroom after the bleeding had stopped, not only my mother was waiting for me but also my father. She had phoned him at the store, and he had rushed home. He scrutinized my face and then signaled for my mother and me to follow him to the kitchen. We sat and he demanded an explanation. So I described how the new guy had been bullying me. Wanting to appear in my father's eyes as entirely blameless, I left out of the description how I had initially provoked the new guy.

He listened and then said coldly, "And you did *nothing* to stop him?"

I started to offer an explanation.

"Nothing!" he interrupted with a grimace of disgust. Turning abruptly to my mother, who all the while was holding her head in her hands, "Look, Mother. Look at your brave son!" he said, sarcastically.

"Please, Chaim," she pleaded. She knew, as I did, that he was near the breaking point.

"Jewish men trembling, hiding under beds while Russian anti-Semites raped and killed their mothers, wives, daughters. Sure, Brushka, encourage him to be a trembling Jew. Don't ever raise your hands in defense. Don't fight back. Mr. Jew-hater, please, please don't hurt me . . ."

He jumped up, touched my shoulder. "Come!" I sensed what he was about to do. So did my mother. "Chaim, don't look for trouble. I beg you."

He didn't respond, didn't look back at her. I followed him.

On the sidewalk, a few houses down the block, my tormentor was swinging a baseball bat, as though simulating batting practice. Father went directly toward him. He seemed surprised to see us. I lagged behind. It was bad enough that my father was there. Now the new guy could tell everyone that I couldn't fight my own battles and had to hide behind my father. But even worse, what if they got into a fistfight? Then people would condemn my father for picking on a school kid.

They stood shoulder to shoulder. In taking up a position to one side of my father, I was struck by the coincidence that he and the new guy were about the same height and build. If they got into a fight and my father was knocked around, the word would get around that not only had his son chickened out after only one punch but his old man had also been badly beaten. After all, he had demonstrated that he knew how to punch while my father, strong as he was, may never have been in a fistfight. Part of me wanted my father to whip the bully in retaliation for the bloodied nose and split lip. On the other hand, if my father were to be beaten easily, after only one or two punches, he would hardly be in a position to criticize me again for not fighting back.

"You did this to my son?" my father began, pointing to my bruised lips.

"What about it?" the bully said, sneering.

"My son says you threw him down on the sidewalk."

"Bullshit! He walked right in front of me. All I did was give him a little push."

My father turned to me, his eyes probed my face. "Does he tell the truth?"

I hesitated, knowing that to reply in the negative would be to incite more harassments in the days ahead.

"He pushed me," I murmured. "And for no reason."

"Bullshit! Crybaby goes running home. Daddy, oh Daddy, help me. A bad, bad boy wants to hurt me." He raised his bat and, as though swatting an insect, swung it over our heads.

"Listen you! No more hitting my son. Or else—"

"Or else what?"

"I'll see to it that you won't hit him again."

"Oh, I'm so, so *scared*."

"I'll talk to your parents."

He held out his bat to my father. "Stick this up you know where."

Instantly my father yanked the bat out of the outstretched hand and then dropped it to the ground. My tormentor blanched, then looked away. Did he see my father as some kind of nut you didn't mess with? He bent, retrieved the bat, and shaking his head as though perplexed, moved off. I wanted to believe he had gotten the message that my father wasn't bluffing.

"Come," my father said and we headed back to our apartment. "You tell me if he bothers you again," he said firmly. I interpreted this to mean that he again would come to my defense. It was the first time he had ever demonstrated that, in his own peculiar way, he cared for me.

Halperin's narrative is quite interesting, and although it took place long ago, bullying incidents just like it occur far too often in schools today. Halperin lets us see why a normally nonviolent boy might pick on another. He was encouraged to continue by another classmate's attention. Also, he quickly digs himself in more deeply than he intended and hopes that a teacher will rescue him. Where is the teacher? Where are the helping witnesses? Why are teachers surprisingly absent when bullying goes on in their classrooms and in the hallways? Where are the student allies? Irving comes from a home where the father is violent. Like Nary from Cambodia, Irving's family had left a repressive homeland where they had lived with state-sanctioned violence. What opportunities did Irving have to use words rather than fists?

Rachel Simmons, in *Odd Girl Out* (2002), writes about the "cult" of popularity and how hard girls have to work to be liked and to fit in. Often, for no reason, they are dropped and their lives become very difficult. Simmons postulates that for girls, bullying often takes place beneath the surface. Adults don't see it and therefore aren't able to pick up on it. But gossiping, starting rumors, and talking behind a person's back are as hurtful as a physical attack. This second account, written by a seventh grader, illustrates the kind of bullying that girls often engage in, playing it out through name-calling, hidden cruelty, and exclusive affiliations.

> Personally I can say that I have been bullied. But also in a sense I can say I'm a bully. Going through schooling you follow everybody's actions. Everybody does [what] they feel is "fitting in." Nobody realizes all the torture a persons feelings go into. When I think about the subject of "talking bad about somebody," it's just what everyone does. Gossip is the biggest deal in the world. Without gossip there would be nothing to explain to your friends. Its hard to explain being a teen, now It makes me mad when I think the world turns its back on me. When a problem occurs you feel like the whole world has gone dark. I have experienced being bullied. There was a time where one of my friends got mad at me and everyone followed with what she was saying. It was hard to sit there and listen to people who don't even know what they are talking about, agree with someone who is wrong. Being wrong is common. Everybody believes what they want to believe. No matter if they know the truth or not, its all in the state of mind. I do not have that bad of experiences. I have always been strong enough to not let what other people think of me, tear me up inside. Its not worth it. Yeah. I do care what people think, but no I'm not going to let it bother me when I know I'm a good person. Teens are teens. Easy as said. In my opinion there is no way to solve bullying. If we get more teachers to watch us, its just going to be a tougher goal for every body to want to bully someone.

As in Halperin's narrative, this girl has both bullied and been a victim of a bully. Gossip, talking behind a person's back, and trying to fit in are all ways that girls experience bullying. Her openness about the difficulty of being a young teenager provides a starting point for further critical literacy work in relation to bullying. Students can generate effective strategies to counter both the more aggressive form of bullying that boys engage in and the more hidden kind that girls often face.

Modeling Conferences

Students need to be taught how to listen and respond to writing authentically. Wait time plays a role here. We all know that if we wait four or five seconds after asking a question, we get more meaningful responses. But it's a little more complicated than that. There are two kinds of wait time: initially holding for a response, certainly, but more important, waiting after a student has started to answer and stops. At that point your first response is most likely to offer verbal encouragement—saying "I know you can do it" or repeating what the student has just said. However, the best thing you can do is nothing: no words, no talking, just quiet. Wait out a child's thinking and you'll get better, more interesting ideas.

Typically, the author begins the conference by saying something like, "This is what I'm writing about and this is where I am now." If appropriate, she might also add, "This is what I need help with." Then the author reads part of the manuscript aloud and her partner asks a number of questions. The author needs to take the time to think of the best answer to a question, which is not necessarily the first one. Silence during a writing conference can be a positive response, because the author is considering the question in order to give it the fullest response. Through writing workshops and bully narratives, the act of bullying is taken seriously. The following chapter shows how bully narratives were incorporated into a seventh-grade language arts classroom.

Chapter Six

Another Model Classroom

Why would the bullies want to kill Freak just for calling them a name? I felt scared for Freak, as if it were really me trying to escape. I don't know what [was] going through their heads. My heart jumped when he pulled out the knife! It's not Freak's fault that he is different. Why can't they just get along? Max is a great person to help Freak and help him out.

—Edwin

Kathleen Jesuskaitis is an extraordinary classroom teacher in Elgin, Illinois, who makes it a point to help her students examine issues of social justice. Kathleen and I worked with her middle school students during the 2002–2003 school year, helping them examine bullying and violence through critical literacy—asking not just what does it mean but is it fair? Throughout the year, we engaged students in discussions of equity and fairness from a variety of perspectives. We also focused on how to make a positive difference.

Short Takes

People feel bullied when they're not allowed to participate fully in life. When a child is made fun of for being himself, he's being bullied. In the fall, we included bullying in a unit on gender issues. As part of the unit, the students studied—and eventually staged—the play *Young Ladies Don't Slay Dragons,* by Joyce Hovelsrud, which questions society's preconceived ideas of the roles females should play within it.

In the spring, a unit on the court system culminated in a mock trial based on the book *Roll of Thunder, Hear My Cry* and its sequel, *Let the Circle .Be Unbroken,* by Mildred Taylor.

The protagonist of these books, Ty Avery, is brutally bullied, put on trial for crimes he didn't commit, and convicted. The students read the first book and then reenacted the trial described in the sequel.

Going Deeper

We examined bullying in greater depth during the winter. First, I spoke to Kathleen's seventh graders about bullying. Then we devoted three class periods to helping students think about related issues. We read *Freak the Mighty*, by Rodman Philbrick, and watched *The Mighty*, the movie made from the book. (The story focuses on Max, a large boy who befriends Kevin, or Freak, a very bright boy who is physically handicapped. Freak is tormented by bullies, as is Kevin. Together, though, they are able to fend them off.) Then the students used a sheet of "bully questions" (see Appendix A) as a springboard for small- and large-group discussions. We also viewed Peter Yarrow's film of his song "Don't Laugh at Me." Finally we asked students to write their own narratives. We invited the students to write anonymously and assured them that they would not be getting anyone in trouble by telling the truth. We explained that we wanted to understand their life through their eyes.

The bully narratives, seventy-two in all, were most revealing about what life in middle school is like, the power inequities, pain, and desperation that children deal with every day in school. We sorted them first by major theme, then broke them into subcategories, looking for ideas that we had missed or that could be classified differently. We eventually identified seven kinds of responses:

- incidents told in the personal voice of the victim
- incidents recounted by bystanders
- "booking" incidents (This was a new term for us. Students described it like this: "When you're booked, someone walks into you and scatters your books and papers across the hall.")

- pieces that focused on what adults *should* do about bullying
- pieces that exposed what adults *don't* do about bullying
- pieces that reflect on "what I should/shouldn't have done" during a bullying incident
- incidents in which the victim or a bystander takes a stand

The Victim's Voice

Many students shared how it felt to be bullied. In the narrative below, the student's choice of words reveals the intensity of his pain:

> I have been bullied many times in school. They would either make fun of me or play a prank on me. Usually I put the ordeal behind me. Othertimes I want to get back at them, make them feel the pain I have had.

Words and phrases like *ordeal, I want to get back at them*, and *feel the pain I have had* indicate just how intense the experience was.

> And listen to this victim:
>   I've been bullied all my life and I take it out on other people and my little brother. When I was bullied it hurt that people were calling me names, picking me last when I was better than somebody else, and people have hit me and pushed me and inc. I don't understand why this has to happen and why it been like that. I think it's because when kids parents divorce they just take the pain out on other people and it isn't right. I wouldn't of taken it out on my brother and other people if this didn't happen. I would have turned out different.

I had been watching this boy throughout our discussions and during his other classroom interactions. He was bright and perceptive—and generally ignored by the other students. "Othered" and excluded, he was trying to make sense of it. He wrote during all the time allotted, even after the bell signaled the end of class. He followed the bully discussion carefully, but spoke little. He was in pain, and wondered, "I don't understand why this has to happen and why it been like that."

Since his parents were divorced, he related bullying to the divorce. But divorce wasn't the real issue.

Another victim shared this story:

> The worst day in my life was when I got bullied by two kids in my school. When it was my first day at my new school I was really nervous because I didn't know anybody. When a couple of weeks passed I kind of got to know a few kids and got some friends. But I don't know couple of my friend started to make fun of me and called me name and they never stopped for a couple of weeks. Then the day came when I had to tell the teacher what was happening to me during Lunch and Gym. The name and things that they called me was that I had headlies, I smell, a quiver. I would like the teacher to have a talk with all the kids in school.

This child was picked on because he was new and also because of his Eastern Asian heritage. He was called a variety of mean names, although he didn't understand that the students had called him *queer*; he thought they said *quiver*. He calls this "the worst day in my life." His pain is visible. In this case, though, the student recognized and trusted adults and turned to them for help. Kathleen was the teacher he turned to. She spoke to the bullies and went to the principal, and the bullying stopped. (The incident, in part, inspired her decision to look more deeply into bullying issues.)

Bystanders

Bystanders observe and report on what happens to children who have been targeted as victims:

> I remember in my elementary years, the popular kids and even the normal kids would always pick on this one girl who was very different. For example one year for hat day, I think it was the 4th grade she wore a hat with Barney on it and everyone made fun of her. Last year she was in my class and these two girls kept making fun of her and once the girl had someone call these two girls Julie and Alyssa and threatened that if they kept teasing her that person would come after them. I guess that's what happens to people when they've been bul-

lied their whole elementary years. At that point Julie and Alyssa were scared and told the principal and the girl got suspended. She moved to a different school. This year she's in a private school.

This was a major theme. A child is picked on because she marches to a different beat. She's aggravated to the point that she threatens the tormentors. Then she's suspended and ends up going to a new school. Initially, the abuse is "under the radar" of the adults. Girls talk and don't talk to the victim in ways adults don't pick up on. But when the victim has finally had enough and threatens to hurt her tormentors physically ("come after them"), the victim herself is the one suspended. Students are very aware of the injustice and lack of protection in schools.

The next narrative is from both a bystander and a victim:

I have witnessed a lot of bullying and even been the victim of bullying. I feel as if I have a lot of friends but still there are a few people who make fun of me for how I look or *how much I weigh*. A lot of the time I will be just sitting there and the person sitting by me in social studies will say your gay! I try not to let it bother me, I just say okay, I'm gay. Then they leave me alone because they think they can't bother me, even though it does a lot. Or sometimes people don't say stuff *to me* but I will be on the bus and hear people saying something and laughing. Most people are nice to me though. It is very hard now to put into words but I just know that I have cried. I have also witnessed bullying, sometimes I try to stop it but other times it's the person who made fun of me so I don't do anything at all. I know that's wrong, but I think they deserve it. I think people should keep their comments to themselves. To keep this school a hate-free place I think that people should keep their comments to themselves, like I said. One more example of being bullied was just yesterday when someone drew a picture of a big circle with a tiny head, feet + hands and said look it is you. That made me feel terrible. I just wish people wouldn't make fun of other people.

Being picked on because of weight was an issue in this seventh grade. So was being called "gay." Seventh graders are more likely to understand the meaning of the word, but students at all grade levels know it's a bad word that is meant to hurt. Whether students are actually gay is not the point. A child who is perceived to be gay or who exhibits any kind of weakness is pounced on. This boy's pain is clear. No student should have to suffer this way in school.

"Booking"

There was a lot of classroom debate about whether or not "booking" constituted bullying. Three quarters of the students felt the practice showed you had friends and was all in good fun. However, some of the students didn't agree:

> Bullying to me means to be hated or picked on or even taunted. I myself have been bullied for four years which is really even shocking to me. Even my friends get bullied!!! Most of my friends are bullies, but I never joined them. I have been picked [on] just for being myself. There isn't even anything wrong about me. I'm just like everyone else. I've even witnessed bullying and booking in the halls or buses. I've even been booked by my own friends!!! I've never done anything to them! I felt so unwanted for nothing! . . . I have never been bullied in this school, which makes me glad and feel safer.

This boy speaks as both a victim and a bystander. He was able to escape rather severe bullying by changing schools. Words and phrases like *hated, taunted,* and *really even shocking to me* drive home just how serious a problem bullying is. "I have been picked [on] just for being myself" is something many victims feel.

Adult Responses

In these seventh graders' narratives, the adults didn't come off as helpful. Students felt that the adults didn't see and didn't protect them:

- "My thoughts were to have more policemen in the halls, more cameras in the halls are ways to make everyone safe in school."

- "My advice would be do what you [adults] say. Your advice works sometimes but you need a new method."
- "I would like the teacher to have a talk with all the kids in school."

Over and over again, students complained about the adults. They did nothing. They didn't protect them. The perpetuators weren't punished.

As adults, what are our responsibilities? It's not enough to educate our students, to add still another subject to the curriculum. These students are right. We have to educate ourselves and change our actions as well. Just as we're asking students to take this seriously, so must we. We need to change our way of dealing with bullying.

For institutional change to occur, all the adults in the school need to work together both to acknowledge bullying as it occurs and to take firm and consistent steps to protect the victims and the allies who report the problems.

Taking a Stand

In the next bystander story, the victim is male and the bystander does something about it:

Every morning this kid Mike is laying on the wood floor of the gym. He minds his own business. I sit there in the gym on the bleachers with my friends and we just hang out until gym starts. Here is the thing the kid Mike lays there and is bothered. Kids push him and throw things at him. They say harsh and cruel things. And this has happened everyday this year. And I've come to my decision that this can't happen any more. People treat him bad for no reason at all. I don't understand why he is bullied. So today I took a stand. It started in gym as usual. I saw Mike getting bullied while he didn't stand up for himself so I approached the situation and told Mike to stand up and the kids to leave. It didn't mean so much to me but that's o.k. I'm just kind of glad Mikes able to do what he wants without being ridiculed. So that's my recent experience. I don't like bullying at all. And bullies should take up a different hobby. Have less tolerance for bullies. I can remember about a million time where I or another have reported bullying and nothing was done. So I think the teachers should do something except telling us what we should do. We handle situations and your tips don't usually work.

This story is significant and representative. The male victim is tormented not only verbally but also physically. However, again it's done without attracting adult attention (though it's hard to understand how teachers can not notice a child who is being harassed daily). Also, since the bullying is done in front of a crowd, the bullies receive an immediate reward. This student is emphatic: "I've come to my decision that this can't happen any more . . . so today I took a stand." This is exactly what we're hoping students will do: that rather than ignore bullying, they'll stand up and make a difference. We encourage students to become allies for one another. Yet this boy also makes it clear that as adults, we're hypocritical. Our advice isn't always helpful, and we don't protect our students. His advice is a wake-up call for us. We need a new method.

The next story is from another ally, a helping witness:

I believe there are two types of bullying; mental bullying and physical bullying. Physical bullying heals over time but the mental bullying stays with you forever. There's a boy in school and he is smart, scrawny and extremely tall. He bullys himself, He calls himself stupid and is always putting himself down and many people go along with it. They think if he makes fun of himself than I can. He doesn't really have many true friends, so I try to be there for him. I think the best thing I can do for him is be his friend and try to build his confidence.

The helping witness is generally an adult. But we can encourage students to act as helping witnesses or allies for their classmates. This author is sensitive to a fellow student with low self-esteem and supports him. How wonderful it would be if all our students helped one another in this way.

Finally, this voice from a bystander who has witnessed a boy being bullied in the gym locker room:

I have seen bullying before in the gym locker room. This happens almost everyday. First, a boy comes into the locker room to change after class. Then a group of boys crowds around him. Finally, while [one] boy holds him down, the others steal his shorts and pull them over his head. Then they all laugh. The first time this happened, I thought it was funny and the boy didn't seem to mind. But then, after the fourth or fifth time I began to feel sad for him. I have stepped in and told the boys to stop. They usually do for about a day but then they keep at it. I wish there was some way to stop this permanently. I can keep a ridicule free zone by treating all of my classmates as equals.

Like Mike, this boy is being repeatedly harassed and humiliated. And this bystander wants the bullying to end permanently. His final sentence shows what he has learned from our work together: the notions of "a ridicule free zone" and "treating all of my classmates as equals" reflect his growing understanding of the issues. He has moved from bystander to ally.

Wider Ramifications

Our work that year had powerful results. The principal wanted all the children in her school to benefit from the effective connections we had made. The following year the faculty labeled the entire school a hate-free zone, and all the teachers worked to help their students use literacy to confront bullying. In particular, as students prepared for their state writing exams, the teachers created prompts that focused on bullying issues.

The bigger issue of how to have safe schools for all children is more difficult to achieve. How can we provide safety and end bullying? is the question all schools must face together.

Afterword: Making a Better and Safer World a Reality

More and more I find myself thinking about the wonderful teachers I've been privileged to know and work with who are representative of all the other fine teachers in our nation's schools. Each year, Mickey Nuccio uses children's literature and critical literacy with her students in Chicago. Ginger Weincek and Kathleen Jesuskaitis continue their classroom antibullying work.

Not long ago I checked in with Sarah, now an eighth grader, whom I first met in Peggy Nadziejko's fifth-grade class in Cicero, Illinois. I asked Sarah if she still visited the nursing home, a practice she'd begun as a fifth grader. She said she did, at least three or four times a week. I was pleasantly surprised and asked her why. She replied: "Because I can brighten their day. My life was darkness until fifth grade. Mrs. Nadziejko made light come into my life. Everything I am today is because of Mrs. Nadziejko. She taught me I can make a difference."

Peggy died an untimely death of cancer, but her work and her spirit live on with her students. I hope all of us can be a similar light in our students' lives as we take a stand against bullying.

Everything I've learned and written about dealing with bullying and harassment depends on accomplished, literate, and compassionate teachers who take a stand, protect the victims, serve as a helping witness for them, and help students become allies for their classmates. Teachers across the globe are engaged in this struggle.

It's time to confront bullying, harassment, and violence whenever and wherever we find it. This can be our contribution. We can make a difference, both in our classrooms and in the world. Every great social movement has been a struggle. Every human right has been fought for; none were simply handed over. If we can change public education to make children truly safe in our schools, all students will finally have the chance to thrive.

As teachers, there are specific things we can do:

- We can announce to our students that bullying will not be tolerated in our classrooms, in the hallways, on the playgrounds, and on school premises.
- We can announce to our students that if anyone has a problem, especially related to bullying, he or she can talk with us after class or send us a note or an email about it.
- We can be helping witnesses to victims of bullying.
- We can immediately take action when bullying, name-calling, or harassment occurs in our presence, publicly identifying it for what it is and making it clear that we will not tolerate it.
- We can use literature, writing, and critical literacy to examine bullying issues in the curriculum.
- We can help students identify themselves as allies for victimized children.
- If students report bullying to us, we can make sure that the bullies are confronted and that the victims, bystanders, and allies feel protected.
- We can work with the other teachers in our school to protect all victims and bystanders from bullying, perhaps by creating a safe-school network.
- We can work within our school district to create safe schools where bullying is never ignored.

Appendix A: Bully Worksheet

The following questions (and others like them) will help students use their critical literacy to think about bullying issues in literature, other texts, movies, and life.

What were the bullying incidents?

For each incident:

- Who were the victims?
- Who were the bullies?
- Who were the innocent bystanders?
- What strategies did the victims use to deal with the bullies?
- Were these strategies effective?
- What other strategies could the victims have used?
- Did anyone else stand up to the bullies?
- Who were the helping witnesses?
- Who were the allies?
- Who else could have been helping witnesses or allies?
- What else could the helping witnesses or allies have done?
- How did family members attempt to help their children deal with the bully issues?

Appendix B

Annotated Book List

Compiled by Roxanne Henkin, Lorri Davis, Jan Dundon and Jessica Williams

African American: Civil Rights and History

Bial, Raymond. 1997. *The Strength of These Arms: Life in the Slave Quarters.* New York: Houghton Mifflin. ISBN: 0395773946. This book details the everyday life of plantation slaves in both text and haunting photographs of recently excavated plantation sites.

Bradley, Marie. 1995. *More Than Anything Else.* New York: Orchard Books. ISBN: 0531087646. Nine-year-old Booker works with his father and brother at the saltworks but dreams of the day when he'll be able to read.

Bridges, Ruby. 1999. *Through My Eyes.* New York: Scholastic. ISBN: 0590189239. Ruby Bridges recounts the story of her involvement, as a six-year-old, in the integration of her school in New Orleans in 1960.

Bullard, Sandra. 1989. *Free at Last: A History of the Civil Rights Movement and Those Who Died in the Struggle.* Montgomery, AL: Teaching Tolerance. ISBN: 0195083814. Provides a history of the Civil Rights Movement.

Coleman, Evelyn. 1996. *White Socks Only.* Morton Grove, IL: Albert Whitman & Company. ISBN: 0807589551. Grandma tells the story about her first trip alone into town during the days when segregation was still in Mississippi.

Coles, Robert. 1995. *The Story of Ruby Bridges.* New York: Scholastic. ISBN: 0590439677. For months, six-year-old Ruby Bridges must confront the hostility of segregationists when she becomes the first African American girl to integrate Frantz Elementary School in New Orleans in 1960 (nonfiction).

Cooper, Floyd. 1998. *Coming Home: From the Life of Langston Hughes*. New York: Puffin. ISBN: 0698116127. This story shows how poet Langston Hughes' experienced racism during his childhood and how it inspired his work.

Curry, Barbara K. and James Michael Brodie. 1996. *Sweet Words So Brave*. Madison, WI: Zino Press Children's Books. ISBN: 1559331798. Filled with photographs and oil paintings. A grandfather tells his granddaughter about the history of African American literature.

Edwards, Pamela Duncan. 1997. *Barefoot: Escape on the Underground*. New York: HarperCollins. ISBN: 0060271388. A heron, a squirrel, a mouse, a deer, and a frog witness a pair of bare feet running frantically through the woods. Eventually Barefoot comes upon a house—but is it really a stop on the Underground Railroad?

Govenar, A. 2000. *Osceola: Memories of a Sharecropper's Daughter*. New York: Hyperion. ISBN: 0786804076. What life was like in the early part of the century as a sharecropper's daughter in Texas.

Hansen, Joyce. 1998. *Women of Hope: African Americans Who Made a Difference*. New York: Scholastic. ISBN: 0590939734. This book includes photographs and biographies of African American women.

Hooks, Williams H. 1996. *Freedom's Fruit*. New York: Alfred A. Knopf. ISBN: 0679924388. Mama Marina is a conjure woman and slave. She is willing to risk all to free her daughter, Sheba.

Livingston, Myra Cohn. 1994. *Keep on Singing: A Ballad of Marian Anderson*. Bridgewater, NJ: Holiday House. ISBN: 0823410986. The life of singer Marian Anderson is portrayed.

Medearis, Angela Shelf. 1995. *The Freedom Riddle*. Birmingham, AL: Lodestar Books. ISBN: 0525674691. It is a Christmas tradition on Master Brown's plantation that when two people see each other in the morning, the first one to say "Christmas gift" receives a present. When Jim, a slave, catches Master Brown in the game, he asks for one thing: that if the master cannot guess Jim's riddle, Jim will win his freedom.

Miller, William. 1998. *The Bus Ride*. NewYork: Lee and Low Books. ISBN: 1880000601. One day Sara decides to see what she's missing by sitting at the back of the bus. The moment she moves up front, she sets off a commotion that reverberates furiously through the city.

———. 1997. *Richard Wright and the Library Card*. New York: Lee and Low Books. ISBN: 1880000571. In the segregated South of the 1920s Richard isn't allowed to borrow books from the library, simply because of the color of his skin.

Mitchell, Margaree King. 1997. *Granddaddy's Gift*. New York: Bridge Water Books. ISBN: 0816764010. When her grandfather registers to vote while living in segregated Mississippi, an African American girl begins to understand why he insists that she attend school.

———. 1998. *Uncle Jed's Barbershop*. New York: Aladdin Paperbacks. ISBN: 0671769693. Despite serious obstacles Uncle Jed, the only black barber in the county, pursues his dream of saving enough money to open his own barbershop.

Myers, Walter Dean. 1997. *Harlem*. New York: Scholastic. ISBN: 0590543407. The words and art in this book capture the flavor of the spirit of Harlem and its music, art, literature, and everyday life.

Parks, Rosa. 1999. *I Am Rosa Parks*. New York: Puffin. ISBN: 0141307102. The autobiography of Rosa Parks.

Ringgold, Faith. 1995. *Aunt Harriet's Underground Railroad in the Sky*. New York: Dragonfly. ISBN: 0517885433. This book follows the path that escaping slaves took on the Underground Railroad.

———. (1996). *Dinner at Aunt Connie's House*. New York: Hyperion. ISBN: 0786811501. This book is about an African American family gathering where framed artwork of famous African American women comes to life and talk about civil rights.

———. 1998. *My Dream of Martin Luther King*. New York: Dragonfly. ISBN: 0517885778. The author talks about a dream she had about the life of Martin Luther King.

———. 1991. *Tar Beach*. New York: Crown Publishers. ISBN: 0517580306. The story of a girl who dreams of flying over her home in Harlem and claiming everything she sees for her family.

Sanders, Scott Russell. 1997. *A Place Called Freedom*. New York: Atheneum Books for Young Readers. ISBN: 0689804709. When young James Sherman and his family are set free, they travel north to Indiana where they build a house, a farm, and a new life for themselves. Inspired by the true story of the founding of Lyles Station, Indiana, this book celebrates the courage, compassion, and wisdom that create nurturing families and strong communities.

Sisulu, Elinor Batexat. 1996. *The Day Gogo Went to Vote*. New York: Little Brown & Company. ISBN: 0316702676. Thembi and her beloved great-grandmother, who has not left the house for many years, go together to vote on the momentous day when Black South Africans are allowed to vote for the first time.

Smalls, Irene. 1995. *Ebony Sea*. New York: Longmeadow Press. ISBN: 068100679X. A beautifully rendered story of the proud Africans known as Ebos and their resistance to slavery in America. The book is a story of loss but also a story of love, courage, and dignity.

Taylor, Mildred. 1999. *The Gold Cadillac*. New York: Scholastic. ISBN: 0590642669. Lois and her family ride from Ohio to Mississippi in their new gold Cadillac. As they drive, they see signs saying, "White only. Colored not allowed." Lois and her sister experience what it's like to be scared because of the color of their skin.

———. 1991. *Roll of Thunder, Hear My Cry*. New York: Scholastic. ISBN: 0590982079. Follows the Logan family and their life in rural Mississippi. This is a classic book.

———. 1991. *Let the Circle Be Unbroken*. New York: Puffin. ISBN: 0140348921. The Logan family watches as their friend is on trial for murder.

Thomas, Velma Maia. 1997. *Lest We Forget: The Passage from Africa to Slavery and Emancipation*. New York: Crown Publishers. ISBN: 0609600303. This book talks about slavery in the United States. It contains replications of authentic documents from history.

———. 2000. *Freedom's Children: The Journey from Emancipation into the Twentieth Century.* New York: Crown Publishers. ISBN: 0609604813. Continues the first book *Lest We Forget* with replications of authentic documents from history during reconstuction.

Tillage, Leon Walter. 1997. *Leon's Story.* New York: Farrar, Straus, Giroux. ISBN: 0374343799. This book is based on a speech that Tillage gives at the school where he works. He grew up as a sharecropper and tells how he was forced to sit in the balcony at the movie theater and hide all night when the Klansmen came riding (nonfiction).

Turner, Robyn Montana. 1993. *Faith Ringgold.* Boston, MA: Little, Brown & Company. ISBN: 0316856525. The life and work of Faith Ringgold is shared.

Wood, Michele. 1996. *Going Back Home: An Artist Returns to the South.* New York: Children's Book Press. ISBN: 0892391979. The author returned to the South to see and feel the land where her ancestors lived. Through the series of paintings and text, the turn-of-the century sharecropping family story is told.

Bullying

Beane, Allan A. 1999. *The Bully Free Classroom: Over 100 Tips and Strategies for Teachers K–8.* Minneapolis, MN: Free Spirit Publishing. ISBN: 1575420546. This book discusses classroom management tips and other helpful ideas to confront bullying.

Bennett, Cherie. 1998. *Life in the Fat Lane.* New York: Laurel Leaf. ISBN: 0440220297. Lara Ardeche thinks she has it made: pretty, great boyfriend, queen of the prom. But when she starts inexplicably gaining weight—and eventually tops 200 pounds—she learns what it is like to be on the wrong side of the scale.

Boyd, Lizi. 1991. *Bailey the Big Bully.* New York: Puffin. ISBN: 0140540512. A group of children invite Bailey the bully to play in their tree house that has a sign saying "No Bullies Allowed!"

Browne, Anthony. 1984. *Willy the Wimp.* New York: Random House. ISBN: 0394870611. A young chimpanzee who is tired of being bullied decides to build up his muscles so he won't be a wimp anymore.

Bunting, Eve. 1995. *Cheyenne Again.* New York: Clarion Books. ISBN: 0395703646. A young Cheyenne boy is taken from his family and is put into an Indian boarding school where he is told to behave like a white person.

Caseley, Judith. 1989. *Ada Potato.* New York: Greenwillow. ISBN: 0688077439. Ada gets the kids who teased her to follow her to school.

Dr. Suess. 1961. *The Sneetches and Other Stories.* New York: Random House Books for Young Readers. ISBN: 0394800893. In this story a star on your belly determines how powerful you are.

Duffey, Betsy. 1993. *How to Be Cool in the Third Grade.* New York: Puffin. ISBN: 0141304669. A story about a boy, bullied at school, who determines that the way not to be bullied is to be cool.

Duncan, Lois. 1990. *Wonder Kid Meets the Evil Lunch Snatcher.* New York: Little Brown & Company. ISBN: 0316195618. Two boys who are bullied develop a character called Wonder Kid to scare off their bully.

Fierstein, Harvey. 2002. *The Sissy Duckling.* New York: Simon & Schuster. ISBN: 0689835663. Elmer the duck is bullied and is made fun of. Eventually he is recognized by his family and friends for his unique self.

Gammell, Stephen. 2000. *Twigboy.* New York: Harcourt. ISBN: 015202137X. Rockwell, a rolling rock, saves Twigboy from being bullied. Together they set out for revenge.

Hahn, Mary Downing. 1991. *Stepping on the Cracks.* New York: Clarion Books. ISBN: 0395585074. In 1944, while her brother is overseas fighting in World War II, Margaret gets a new view of the school bully, Gordy, when she finds him hiding his own brother, an army deserter, and decides to help him.

Hayes, Daniel. 1995. *The Trouble with Lemons.* New York: Archway Paperback. ISBN: 0449704165. His real name was Tyler but he felt like a lemon. One night he and a friend went swimming at the forbidden quarry and found a dead body.

Howe, James. 1996. *Pinky and Rex and the Bully.* New York: Atheneum. ISBN: 0689800215. A boy wonders how he fits in after a bully makes fun of him for liking the color pink and playing with girls.

Jian, Ji-Li; and David Henry Hwang. 1998. *Red Scarf Girl: A Memoir of the Cultural Revolution*. New York: Harper Trophy. ISBN: 0064462090. Ji-Li tells the story of her life as it is completely torn apart by the Cultural Revolution and her own thoughts and beliefs on Chinese Communism. She watches in terror as her favorite teachers are being harassed at school, people's homes are ransacked, and her father is humiliated.

Johnson, J. 1999. *How Do I Feel About Bullies and Gangs?* London: The Watts Publishing Group. ISBN: 0749636289. This book encourages children to say how they feel about issues that affect them.

Koja, Kathe. 2003. *Buddha Boy*. New York: Farrar, Straus and Giroux. ISBN: 0374309981. Justin's growing friendship with Jinsen "Buddha Boy" is complicated because of the bullying that Jinsen endures for being different.

Knight, Margy Burns. 1993. *Who Belongs Here? An American Story*. Gardiner, ME: Tilbury House. ISBN: 0884881581. Based on a true story, young readers are invited to explore the human implications of intolerance. Anecdotes relating the experiences of refugees and their contributions to American culture are incorporated.

Krensky, Stephen. 1998. *Louise Takes Charge*. New York: Dial Books for Young Readers. ISBN: 0803723067. Louise organizes a group of kids to be apprentices to Jasper the bully.

Kulkin, S. 1993. *Speaking out. Teenagers Take on Race, Sex, and Identity*. New York: G.P. Putnam's Sons. ISBN: 0399223436. Case studies of young adults' experiences with bullying and harassing.

Mead, Alice. 2000. *Junebug and the Reverend*. New York: Farrar Straus Giroux. ISBN: 0440415713. Having moved out of the housing project and into a new home along with his mother and sister, Junebug discovers that bullies are everywhere and that the elderly can make great friends.

Miklowitz, G. D. 1985. *The War Between Classes*. New York: Bantam Doubleday Dell Books for Young Readers. ISBN: 0440994063. Amy, a Japanese girl, and Adam, a Caucasian boy, are dating. Neither one of their parents will accept their relationship. Now they are involved in a school experiment designed to make students aware of their prejudices.

Naylor, Phyllis Reynolds. 1994. *The King of the Playground*. New York: Aladdin Library. ISBN: 0689718020. After being bullied for years, a friendship is forming between Kevin and his bully Sammy.

Nickle, John. 1999. *The Ant Bully*. New York: Scholastic. ISBN: 0590395912. Lucas, who bullies ants, falls down the ant hole and finds out what it's like to be bullied.

Oram, Hiawyn. 1993. *Angry Arthur*. New York: Random House Children's Books. ISBN: 0099196611. Amazing things happen when Arthur gets mad.

Passen, Lisa. 1991. *Fat, Fat, Rose Marie*. New York: Henry Holt & Company. ISBN: 0805016538. A story about a new girl in school who is overweight and teased relentlessly by a thin girl.

Petty, Kate. 1991. *Being Bullied*. New York: Barrons Juveniles. ISBN: 0812046617. After being bullied by a girl at school, Rita finds the courage to stand up to her bully.

Philbrick, Rodman. 1999. *Freak the Mighty*. New York: Econo-Clad Books. ISBN: 0785765948. This book is about the friendship between Kevin "Freak," a brilliant 12-year-old whose birth defect prevents growth, and gigantic Max. Together they find the courage to confront violence and bullies and rebuild their lives. The video version of this book, *The Mighty* is also well done.

Polacco, Patricia. 1998. *My Rotten Redheaded Older Brother*. New York: Simon & Schuster Books for Young Readers. ISBN: 0689820364. Tells the tale of a girl who wishes on a shooting star to do something better than her bratty older brother.

———. 1998. *Thank You Mr. Falker*. New York: Philomel Books. ISBN: 0399231668. A new teacher is the only person who will take the time to help a young dyslexic girl learn to read.

Poulet, Virginia and Donald Charles. 1971. *Blue Bug and the Bullies*. Danbury, CT: Children's Press. ISBN: 0516034189. A description of blue bug's reactions to his bullies.

Powell, Jillian. 1999. *Talking About Bullying*. New York: Raintree/Steck Vaughn. ISBN: 0817255354. A discussion about bullying.

Romain, Trevor. 1997. *Bullies Are a Pain in the Brain*. Minneapolis, MN: Free Spirit Publishing. ISBN: 1575420236. This book gives advice on how to deal with being bullied.

Rowling, J. K. 2003. *Harry Potter and the Order of the Phoenix*. New York: Scholastic. ISBN: 043935806X. Also by J. K. Rowling: *Harry Potter and the Sorcerer's Stone; Harry Potter and the Chamber of Secrets; Harry Potter and the Prisoner of Azkaban;* and *Harry Potter and the Goblet of Fire*. All of the Harry Potter books and movies provide specific instances of bullying. Harry himself is bullied for being different. Due to the popularity of these books, bully issues can be discussed in book groups.

Tolan, S. S. 1990. *Plague Year*. New York: William Morrow & Company. ISBN: 0688088015. Bran has been hiding a terrible secret. Now that it's out, the town wants him gone.

Wilhelm, Hans. 2001. *Tyrone the Horrible*. New York: Scholastic. ISBN: 0439993431. A tale about a young dinosaur who outsmarts the swamp bully.

Winthrop, Elizabeth. 1992. *Luke's Bully*. New York: Puffin. ISBN: 0670831034. Luke discovers that Arthur, who picks on Luke, isn't so bad and they become friends.

Voigt, Cynthia. 1996. *Bad Girls*. New York: Scholastic. ISBN: 0590601342. Michelle and Mickey team up to effectively deal with the class bully. A story of two girls who don't take things lying down and aren't afraid of anything.

Yep, Laurence. 2000. *Cockroach Cooties*. New York: Hyperion. ISBN: 0786804874. Streetwise Teddy usually stays out of sight of the bully nicknamed Arniezilla. However, when his sickly sweet little brother, Bobby, insults Arnie, Teddy must reluctantly come to the rescue and become the target of Arnie's wrath instead.

Death and Aging

Atkins, J. 1999. *A Name on the Quilt: A Story of Remembrance*. New York: Atheneum Books for Young Readers. ISBN: 0689815921. Lauren misses her Uncle Ron and makes a panel for the quilt.

Brown, Marc, and Laurie Krasny Brown. 1996. *When Dinosaurs Die: A Guide to Understanding Death.* New York: Little Brown. ISBN: 0316119555. Gently explains death to children.

Bunting, Eve. 2000. *Can You Do This, Old Badger?* Orlando, FL: Harcourt. ISBN: 0152016546. Even though Old Badger cannot do some things with ease anymore, he can still teach Little Badger how to stay safe and be happy.

Clifford, Eth. 1985. *The Remembering Box.* Boston: Houghton Mifflin. ISBN: 0688117775. Joshua's weekly visits to his grandma on the Jewish Sabbath give him an understanding of tradition that helps him accept her death.

De Paola, Tomie. 1973. *Nana Upstairs & Nana Downstairs.* New York: Puffin. ISBN: 0140502904. A young boy enjoys the relationships he has with his grandmother and his great-grandmother, but learns to face their inevitable death.

———. 1981. *Now One Foot, Now the Other.* New York: G. P. Putnam's Sons. ISBN: 0399207740. Bobby teaches his grandfather to walk after he suffers from a stroke.

Fox, Mem. 1989. *Wilfrid Gordon McDonald Partridge.* Brooklyn, NY: Kane/Miller Book Publishers. ISBN: 0916291049. A young boy strives to discover the meaning of memory to help restore that of an elderly friend.

Kinsey-Warnock, Natalie. 1989. *The Canada Geese Quilt.* New York: Penguin Books. ISBN: 0440407192. A young girl is feeling lost and alone when her grandmother suffers a stroke.

Varley, Susan. 1984. *Badger's Parting Gifts.* New York: Mulberry Books. ISBN: 0688115187. Badger's friends are sad when he dies but they treasure the legacies he left them.

Wild, Margaret. 1990. *Remember Me.* St. Morton Grove, IL: Albert Whitman & Company. ISBN: 0807569348. Elle's grandma may forget many things, but she remembers the special times they have shared.

Woodson, Jacqueline. 2000. *Sweet, Sweet Memory.* New York: Hyperion Books for Children. ISBN: 0786802413. A young girl and her grandmother are sad because Grandpa dies, but feel better when funny memories of him make them laugh.

Families

Cha, Dia. 1996. *Dia's Story Cloth: The Hmong People's Journey of Freedom.* New York: Lee & Low Books. ISBN: 1880000342. This is the story about the Hmong people's journey to freedom.

Dooley, Nora. 2002. *Everybody Brings Noodles.* Minneapolis, MN: Carolrhoda Books. ISBN: 0876144555. While organizing a neighborhood Fourth of July party, Carrie finds out that everyone is bringing noodles, her favorite food. Each culture shares how they prepare noodles.

Erlbach, Arlene. 1996. *The Families Book: True Stories About Real Kids and the People They Live with and Love.* Minneapolis, MN: Free Spirit Publishing. ISBN: 1575420023. This book talks about family life and how relatives interact.

Fox, Mem. 1997. *Whoever You Are.* New York: Harcourt Brace & Company. ISBN: 0152007873. People across the world are both the same and different.

Garza, Carmen Lomas. 1990. *Family Pictures: Cuadros de Familia.* San Francisco, CA: Children's Book Press. ISBN: 0892390506. A description of the author's experiences growing up in Kingsville, Texas.

Gilman, Phoebe. 1992. *Something from Nothing.* New York: Scholastic. ISBN: 0590472801. Joseph's grandfather transforms a blanket he made for him into a jacket, vest, a tie, a handkerchief, and a button after it becomes old and tattered.

Jenness, Aylete. 1990. *Families: A Celebration of Diversity, Commitment, and Love.* New York: Houghton Mifflin. ISBN: 0395470382. Descriptions of many kinds of families.

Nye, Naomi Shihab. 1994. *Sitti's Secrets.* New York: Four Winds Press. ISBN: 0027684601. A girl misses her grandmother and remembers her visit to her grandmother's Palestinian village.

Say, Allen. 1993. *Grandfather's Journey.* New York: Houghton Mifflin. ISBN: 0395570352. The author tells about his grandfather's life in America and Japan.

Skutch, Robert. 1995. *Who's in a Family?* Berkeley, CA: Tricycle Press. ISBN: 188367266X. This book talks about diversity in families.

Feeling Different

Baumann, Kurt. 1993. *The Hungry One*. New York: North-South Books. ISBN: 1558581219. A strange tale about greed and the factors that lead to it.

Bertrand, Diane. 1999. *Trino's Choice*. Houston, TX: Piñata Books. ISBN: 1558852689. Nothing in Trino's life is going right. When he hides from bullies in a bookstore, he begins to find his place in life.

Bloor, Edward. 1997. *Tangerine*. New York: Scholastic. ISBN: 059043277X. Paul, a legally blind boy, discovers the truth about his football star older brother.

Cannon, Janell. 1993. *Stellaluna*. San Diego, CA: Harcourt. ISBN: 0152802177. A baby bat is adopted by a family of birds after she is knocked out of her mother's grasp by an owl.

———. 2000. *Crickwing*. New York: Harcourt. ISBN: 0152017909. A lonely cockroach named Crickwing saves the day for the leaf-cutting ants when their enemies attack.

Farrell, Ryan C. 1998. *God Made Me Special!!!! Tourette Syndrome. My Personal Story*. New York: Rasberry Publications. ISBN: 1884825222. Ryan was diagnosed with Tourette syndrome in 1994. He suffers with tics, obsessive-compulsive behaviors, ADHD and conduct disorder. Ryan struggles with being teased and frustrated.

Gantos, Jack. 1998. *Joey Pigza Swallowed the Key*. New York: HarperTrophy. ISBN: 0064408337. A story about a boy with ADHD. When his medications wear off, he starts acting weird.

———. 2000. *Joey Pigza Loses Control*. New York: HarperTrophy. ISBN: 0064410226. A boy who is taking medication for ADHD goes to spend the summer with his alcoholic father who he doesn't really know. He tries to help the baseball team his father coaches win the championship.

Hill, David. 1997. *Fat, Four-Eyed and Useless*. New York: Scholastic. ISBN: 1869432800. A boy named Max who thinks he is useless has finally found something he's good at.

Gilson, Jamie. 2002. *Stink Alley*. New York: HarperCollins. ISBN: 0060292172. In 1614, orphan Lizzy Tinker lives in Holland with the English Pilgrims who would eventually move to America. She struggles with fitting in and finding her way.

Holt, Kimberly Willis. 1999. *When Zachary Beaver Came to Town*. New York: Henry Holt & Company. ISBN: 0805061169. When Zachary Beaver comes to Antler as part of a traveling sideshow, Toby begins to realize that there might just be people who have it worse than him. By reaching out to Zachary in small ways, Toby is better able to put his own problems into perspective.

Polacco, Patricia. 1998. *Thank You Mr. Falker*. New York: Philomel Books. ISBN: 0399231668. A new teacher is the only person who will take the time to help a young dyslexic girl learn to read.

Hearing Students' Voices

Birdseye, Debbie Holsclaw, and Tom Birdseye. 1997. *Under Our Skin: Kids Talk About Race*. Bridgewater, NJ: Holiday House. ISBN: 82341325X. Six students aged twelve to thirteen discuss how the traditions of their ethnic backgrounds affect their daily life.

Holliday, Laurel. 2000. *Why Do They Hate Me? Young Lives Caught in War and Conflict*. New York: Archway. ISBN: 0671034545. In three sections about Northern Ireland, Israel and Palestine, and the Holocaust and World War II, children speak in secret diaries, letters, essays, and memoirs.

Leigh, Nila K. 1993. *Learning to Swim in Swaziland: A Child's-Eye View of a Southern African Country*. New York: Scholastic. ISBN: 0590459384. An eight-year-old girl, Nila, describes her year living in Swaziland. She shares her collection of letters.

Roberts-Davis, Tanya. 2001. *We Need to Go to School: Voices of the Rugmark Children*. Toronto, ON, Canada: Groundwood Books/Douglas & McIntyre. ISBN: 0888994257. Nepalese children's voices of their lives. They formerly worked in carpet factories.

Shea, Pegi Deitz. 1995. *The Whispering Cloth*. Honesdale, PA: Boyds Mills Press. ISBN: 1563971348. Little Mai wished she could stitch a beautiful pa'ndau herself, but what story could she tell?

Strom, Yale. 1996. *Quilted Landscape: Conversations with Young Immigrants*. New York: Simon & Schuster Children's Publishing.

ISBN: 0689800746. Twenty-six young people of different ages and nationalities describe their experience of leaving their countries and immigrating to the United States.

Hispanic

Bunting, Eve. 1996. *Going Home*. New York: HarperCollins. ISBN: 006026296. Although a Mexican family comes to the United States to work as farm laborers so that their children will have opportunities, the parents still consider Mexico their home.

Cisneros, Sandra. 1994. *Hairs Pelitos*. New York: Alfred A. Knopf. ISBN: 0679861718. A child describes how each person in the family has hair that looks and acts differently.

Dorros, Arthur. 1991. *Abuela*. New York: Dutton Children's Press. ISBN: 0525447504. While riding on a bus with her grandmother, a little girl imagines that they are carried up into the sky and fly over the sights of New York City. They narrate their journey in English with Spanish phrases.

Elya, Susan. 2002. *Home at Last*. New York: G. P. Putnam's Sons. ISBN: 1584300205. Ana Patino helps Mama by translating English for her. Mama decides to take English lessons as she learns to feel at home in her new country.

Jimenez, Francisco. 1997. *The Circuit. Stories from the Life of a Migrant Child*. Boston, MA: Houghton Mifflin. ISBN: 0395070021. This is Mr. Jimenez's story of his childhood. This is moving and inspiring.

———. 1998. *La Mariposa*. Boston: Houghton Mifflin. ISBN: 0618073475. First-grader Francisco can only speak Spanish. The migrant worker's son has trouble in first grade. The classroom caterpillar makes a difference.

———. 2001. *Breaking Through*. Boston, MA: Houghton Mifflin. ISBN: 0618011730. The continuation of his life from *The Circuit*. Mr. Jimenez is now a professor at Santa Clara University.

Johnston, Tony. 1996. *My Mexico—México mi'o*. New York: G. P. Putnam's Sons. ISBN: 0399222758. The book is a collection of poems about the spirit of Mexico.

———. 2001. *Any Small Goodness: A Novel of the Barrio*. New York: The Blue Sky Press. ISBN: 0439189365. The life of eleven-year-old Arturo Rodriguez as he grows up in a warm and happy family in the barrio of East Los Angeles.

Mora, Pat. 1994. *Pablo's Tree*. New York: Macmillan. ISBN: 0027674010. The special relationship between Pablo and his grandfather is shared on Pablo's birthday.

Ryan, Pam Munoz. 2000. *Esperanza Rising*. New York: Scholastic. ISBN: 043912042X. Esperanza's wonderful life on her family's ranch in Mexico ends as they flee to a camp for migrant workers in California during the Depression. She copes with and survives the changes.

Soto, Gary. 1993. *Too Many Tamales*. New York: G. P. Putnam's Sons. ISBN: 03999221468. Maria tries on her mother's wedding ring while helping make tamales for a Christmas family get-together. Panic ensues when hours later, she realizes the ring is missing.

Torros, Leyla. 1995. *Saturday Sancocho*. New York: Farrar, Straus, Giroux. ISBN: 0374464510. Every Saturday Maria Lili looks forward to making chicken sancocho and then one Saturday there are no eggs.

Immigration

Bunting, Eve. 1988. *How Many Days to America? A Thanksgiving Story*. Boston, MA: Houghton Mifflin. ISBN: 0395547776. Refugees from a Caribbean island embark on a dangerous boat trip to America where they have a special reason to celebrate.

Hest, Amy. 1997. *When Jessie Came Across the Sea*. Cambridge, MA: Candlewick Press. ISBN: 076361274X. The story of our immigrant heritage as Jessica travels across the ocean to a new life and love. The book transcends time and culture in a tribute to the courage and hope of all who seek a better life.

Lawlor, Veronica. 1995. *I Was Dreaming to Come to America: Memories from the Ellis Island Oral History Project*. New York: Penguin Group. ISBN: 0670861642. Here is a collection from some of the people, mostly children at the time, who passed through Ellis Island between 1900 and 1925.

Knight, Margy Burns. 1993. *Who Belongs Here? An American Story*. Gardiner, ME: Tilbury House. ISBN: 0884481107. Based on a true story, young readers are invited to explore the human implications of intolerance. Anecdotes relating the experiences of refugees and their contributions to American culture are incorporated.

Strom, Yale. 1996. *Quilted Landscape: Conversations with Young Immigrants.* New York: Simon & Schuster Children's Publishing. ISBN: 0689800746. Twenty-six young people of different ages and nationalities describe their experience of leaving their countries and immigrating to the United States.

Impact of War

Adler, David A. 1987. *The Number on My Grandfather's Arm.* New York: UAHC Press. ISBN: 0807403288. A dialogue and photographic display between a young girl and her grandfather, a Polish-born Holocaust survivor. The grandfather shares his experiences as a young man in Poland and in the Auschwitz concentration camp.

Bunting, Eve. 1998. *So Far from the Sea.* New York: Clarion Press. ISBN: 0395720958. When seven-year-old Laura and her family visit Grandfather's grave at the Manzanar War Relocation Center, the Japanese American child leaves behind a symbol.

Coerr, Eleanor. 1993. *Sadako.* New York: G. P. Putnam's Sons. ISBN: 0399217711. Coerr tells the moving true story of Sadako and her brave struggle against leukemia, the "atom-bomb disease," which she developed when she was twelve, just ten years after Hiroshima.

Crew, Gary and Shaun Tan, Illustrator. 2000. *Memorial.* Port Melbourne, Victoria, Australia: Thomas C. Lothian. ISBN: 0850919835. This story about a tree brings forth memories of war.

Hoelstlandt, Jo. 1993. *Star of Fear, Star of Hope.* New York: Walker and Company. ISBN: 0802783732. Nine-year-old Helen is confused by the disappearance of her Jewish friend during the German occupation of Paris.

Innocenti, Roberto. 1985. *Rose Blanche.* Mankato, MN: Creative Education. ISBN: 1556702078. During World War II, Rose

Blanche follows a truck out of town to a forest clearing where she discovers a concentration camp with hungry, cold children huddled behind a barbed wire fence.

Jakes, John. 1986. *Susanna of the Alamo: A True Story*. Orlando, FL: Harcourt Brace Jovanovich. ISBN: 0152005927. Talks about the experiences of a Texas woman and her baby who survived the 1836 massacre at the Alamo.

Kodama, Tatsuharu. 1992. *Shin's Tricyle*. New York: Walker and Company. ISBN: 0802783759. Fifty years after the bombing of Hiroshima, the true story is shared of Nobuo Tetsutani and his beloved son, Shin, whose life was tragically cut short by the atomic blast. Rich, stirring illustrations will move the hearts of children and adults. Shin's memory lives on through the tricycle now permanently displayed in the Hiroshima Peace Museum.

Kogawa, J. 1982. *Itsuka*. New York: Doubleday. ISBN: 0385468865. One Canadian Japanese family's story about their relocation during World War II.

———. 1992. *Obasan*. New York: Doubleday. ISBN: 0385468865. The continuing story of the family after World War II and the decades-long work Aunt Emily undertook trying to get an official apology from the Canadian government.

Lowry, Lois. 1989. *Number the Stars*. Boston, MA: Houghton Mifflin. ISBN: 0395510600. Ten-year-old Annemarie is best friends with Jewish Ellen in Denmark during World War II. Annemarie helps save Ellen and her family.

Maruki, Toshi. 1980. *Hiroshima No Pika*. New York: Lothrop, Lee & Shepard Books. ISBN: 068812973. A retelling of a mother's account of what happened to her family during the flash that destroyed Hiroshima in 1945.

Nerlove, Miriam. 1996. *Flowers on the Wall*. New York: McElderry Books. ISBN: 0395570352. A young Jewish girl living in Nazi-occupied Warsaw struggles to survive with her family by drawing on her dingy apartment walls.

Noguchi, Rick, and Deneen Jenks. 2001. *Flowers from Mariko*. New York: Lee & Low Books. ISBN: 1584300329. Mariko plants a garden to raise the spirits of her family after they have been released from the Japanese American internment camp.

Polacco, Patricia. 1994. *Pink and Say*. New York: Philomel Books. ISBN: 0399226710. Say Curtis describes his meeting with a black soldier during the Civil War and their capture by Southern troops.

———. 2000. *The Butterfly*. New York: Philomel Books. ISBN: 0399231706. In France, during World War II, Monique's mother hides a Jewish girl.

Sim, Dorrith M. 1996. *In My Pocket*. San Diego, CA: Harcourt Brace. ISBN: 0152013571. Fear and uncertainty afflict everyone on the boat on the morning in July 1939 when Jewish children sail from Holland to the safety of a new life in Scotland.

Tsuchiya, Yukio. 1988. *Faithful Elephants: A True Story of Animals, People, and War*. Boston, MA: Houghton Mifflin. ISBN: 0395465559. Recounts how three elephants in a Tokyo Zoo were put to death because of the war, focusing on the pain shared by the elephants and the keepers who must starve them.

Uchida, Yoshiko. 1985. *Journey to Topaz*. Berkeley, CA: Creative Arts Book Company. ISBN: 0916870855. Eleven-year-old Yuki Sakane is sent to the Japanese internment camp named Topaz. The story of *The Bracelet* comes from this book.

———. 1993. *The Bracelet*. New York: Philomel Books. ISBN: 039922503X. Uchida draws on her own childhood as a Japanese American during World War II to tell the poignant story of a young girl's discovery of the power of memoir. A seven-year-old is sent with her family to the internment camp.

Wild, Margaret, and Julie Vivas. 1991. *Let the Celebrations Begin!* New York: Orchard Books. ISBN: 0531085376. A child who remembers life at home before life in a concentration camp makes toys with the women to give to the other children at the party they are going to have when the soldiers arrive to liberate the camp.

Yolen, Jane. 1988. *The Devil's Arithmetic*. New York: Penguin Group. ISBN: 0142401099. A seventh grader opens the door for Elijah during Passover and is transformed back to the Holocaust living her aunt's life.

Multicultural

Ada, Alma Flor. 1997. *Gathering the Sun*. New York: Lothrop, Lee & Shepard Books. ISBN: 0688139035. The author has written twenty-eight poems that celebrate honor and pride, family and friends, history and heritage, and the bounty of the harvest.

Angelou, Maya. 1994. *My Painted House, My Friendly Chicken, and Me*. New York: Crown Books for Young Readers. ISBN: 0517596679. The story of an eight-year-old Ndebele girl who lives in a village in South Africa with her mother, aunts, sisters, mischievous brother, and her best friend, a chicken.

Breckler, Rosemary. 1996. *Sweet Dried Apples, A Vietnamese Wartime Childhood*. Boston, MA: Houghton Mifflin. ISBN: 039573570X. A Vietnamese child remembers wartime and her relationship with her grandfather, the village herb doctor.

Brenner, Barbara. 2000. *Voices: Poetry and Art from Around the World*. Washington, DC: National Geographic Society. ISBN: 0792270711. A collection of works from around the world.

Chen, Da. 2001. *China's Son: Growing Up in the Cultural Revolution*. New York: Delacorte Press. ISBN: 0385729294. Da Chen's family is in trouble during the cultural revolution in China.

Choi, Sook Nyui. 1991. *Year of Impossible Goodbyes*. New York, Bantam Doubleday Dell. ISBN: 0440407591. A ten-year-old girl talks about the experience of her Korean family during the Japanese occupation as World War II ends.

———. 1993. *Echoes of the White Giraffe*. New York: Bantam Doubleday Dell. ISBN: 0440409705. A fifteen-year-old girl is living in a refugee camp in Pusan where she tries to rebuild a normal life.

Fishman, Cathy Goldberg. 1997. *On Rosh Hashanah and Yom Kippur*. New York: Aladdin Library. ISBN: 0689805268. How can you tell when it is time for Rosh Hashanah and Yom Kippur? The author's gentle narrative introduces readers to all the meaningful symbols of the High Holy Days.

Huong, Duong Thu. 1988. *Paradise of the Blind*. New York: Penguin Books. ISBN: 0688114458. A story of three Vietnamese women trying to survive in a society where subservience to men is the norm and corruption ruins every dream.

Johnson, Dolores. 1994. *Seminole Diary: Remembrances of a Slave.* New York: Macmillan. ISBN: 00207478483. Libbie and her family moved to the Seminole village and worked side by side with the tribe members. But that good life was not to last, as the white man tried to take the Seminole land away. Should they flee farther south into South Florida's swamps or relocate to Oklahoma?

Kherdian, David. 1979. *The Road from Home: The Story of an Armenian Girl.* New York: Puffin. ISBN: 0140325247. A biography of the author's mother with a concentration on her childhood in Turkey before the Turkish government deported the Armenian population.

Knight, Margy Burns. 1992. *Talking Walls.* New York: Henry Holt & Company. ISBN: 0884481026. An illustrated description of walls around the world and their significance, from the Great Wall of China to the Berlin Wall.

Lanier, Shannon, and Jane Feldman. 2000. *Jefferson's Children: The Story of One American Family.* New York: Random House. ISBN: 0375905979. A story about the multiracial family of Thomas Jefferson. One of Thomas Jefferson's descendents through Sally Hemmings contacts and visits as many descendants of Thomas Jefferson as possible. Their stories are interesting and diverse.

Little, Mimi. 1996. *Yoshino and the Foreigner.* New York: Farrar, Straus, & Giroux. ISBN: 0374324484. A true story of how an American soldier learned Japanese customs as he fell in love with his future wife.

Pak, Soyung. 2002. *A Place to Grow.* New York: Arthur A. Levine. ISBN: 0439130158. A true story of a family's journey from South Korea to the United States to be able to plant the "garden of their heart."

Ringgold, Faith. 2002. *Cassie's World Quilt.* New York: Random House. ISBN: 0375812008. This story talks about the people and things that make a girl's surroundings special.

Rippin, Sally. 1996. *Speak Chinese, Fang Fang.* Norwood, South Australia: Scholastic Australian Group. ISBN: 1862912904. Fang Fang moves from China to Australia, and although she understands Chinese, she is hesitant to speak it.

Rosen, Michael. 1992. *Elijah's Angel.* San Diego, CA: Harcourt Brace. ISBN: 0152253947. At Christmas-Hanukkah time, a Christian woodcarver gives a carved angel to a young Jewish friend who struggles with accepting the Christmas gift until he realizes that friendship means the same thing in any religion.

Smith, David J. 2002. *If the World Were a Village: A Book About the World's People.* Tonawanda, NY: Kids Can Press. ISBN: 1550747797. This book imagines the world as a village of one hundred people and provides statistics on food, population, languages, and so on.

Staples, Suzanne Fisher. 1989. *Shabanu: Daughter of the Wind.* New York: Random House. ISBN: 0679810307. A young Pakistani woman is faced with a tough decision. Should she uphold her family's honor or listen to her heart?

———. 1993. *Haveli.* New York: Random House. ISBN: 0679865691. A continuation of *Shabanu: Daughter of the Wind.* A young Pakistani woman struggles against the traditions of the past.

Tucker, Alan. 1999. *Side by Side.* Norwood, South Australia: Omnibus Books. ISBN: 1862913110. The history of the Europeans coming to Australia is written in text and beautifully illustrated through maps. Both the peaceful and violent stories are told.

Utemorrah, Daisy. 1992. *Do Not Go Around the Edges.* Broome, Western Australia: Magabala Books Aboriginal Corporation. ISBN: 0958810117. Each page has both the text of Daisy, an Australian Aboriginal woman, and one of her poems. Her story is dramatic, and the accompanying pictures feature Aboriginal motifs.

Woodson, Jacqueline. 2001. *The Other Side.* New York: G. P. Putnam's Sons. ISBN: 0399231161. The story of two girls, one white and the other black, who befriend each other and sit on the fence that divides the town they live in.

Wong, Janet S. 2002. *Apple Pie 4th of July*. New York: Harcourt. ISBN: 015202543X. A Chinese American child is surprised when people choose Chinese food for their Fourth of July meal.

Social Issues

Bauer, Marion (ed.). 1994. *Am I Blue?* New York: HarperCollins. ISBN: 0064405877. Well-respected children's authors write stories that include a gay or lesbian character or issue. In the title story a young boy is beaten up because he is perceived to be gay. For one day, people turn blue if they are gay. The results are surprising.

Bunting, Eve. 1989. *The Wednesday Surprise*. New York: Clarion Books. ISBN: 0395559626. A father and son live in an airport.

———. 1994. *A Day's Work*. New York: Clarion Books. ISBN: 0395673216. Francisco lies that his grandfather is a gardener to get work. His Abuelo teaches him a lesson about the truth.

———. 1994. *Smoky Night*. New York, Harcourt Brace. ISBN: 0152018840. A boy and his mother learn the value of getting along with others from different backgrounds during the Los Angeles riots.

———. 1999. *The Blue and the Gray*. New York: Scholastic. ISBN: 0590601970. Two young children explore the fields beyond a construction site where their new homes are being built. In 1862, this was a battleground for the Civil War. In counterpoint, the destruction and misery of the Civil War is contrasted with the modern interracial community.

Chambers, Veronica. 1998. *Amistad Rising: A Story of Freedom*. New York: Harcourt Brace. ISBN: 0152018034. Based on the true story of Joseph Cinque, a young man kidnapped from his homeland and imprisoned on the slave ship, Amistad.

Crump, Barry. 1999. *The Pungapeople of Ninety Mile Beach*. Microdot, Aukland, New Zealand: Hodder Moa Beckett Publishers. ISBN: 1869587782. A story about how the Pungapeople of New Zealand outwit their foes to save their land from pollution.

Curtis, Christopher Paul. 1999. *Bud, Not Buddy.* New York: Delacorte Press. ISBN: 0385323069. During the Depression, ten-year-old Bud goes looking for his father.

Ewing, Lynne. 1996. *Drive-By.* New York: HarperCollins. ISBN: 0060271256. A story about a boy struggling to find his way after his older brother is killed in a gang-related shooting.

Grant, Reg. 2000. *Amnesty International.* Danbury, CT: Franklin Watts. ISBN: 0531146197. A book about human rights.

————. 2001. *World Organizations: Amnesty International.* Danbury, CT: Franklin Watts. ISBN: 0531148114. Nonfiction book that describes the work of Amnesty International.

Heron, Ann, and Meredith Maran. 1991. *How Would You Feel If Your Dad Was Gay?* Boston: Alyson. ISBN: 1555831885. Jasmine and her older brother Michael live with their father and Andrew. When Jasmine shares her home life with her class, her brother has to deal with the consequences in his junior high school. The family works together to educate their community and continue to love each other.

Kroloff, Rabbi Charles A. 1993. *54 Ways You Can Help the Homeless.* West Orange, NJ: Behrman House. Southport, CT: Hugh Levin Associates. ISBN: 0883638886. This book offers suggestions on how to offer aid to this population.

Lewis, Barbara. 1995. *The Kid's Guide to Service Projects.* Minneapolis, MN: Free Spirit Publishing, Inc. ISBN: 0915793822. Many wonderful service projects are described in detail.

Lorbiecki, Marybeth. 1998. *Sister Anne's Hands.* New York: Dial Books for Young Readers. ISBN: 0803720394. A seven-year-old has her first encounter with racism when an African American nun comes to teach at her parochial school.

McGovern, Ann. 1997. *The Lady in the Box.* New York: Turtle Books. ISBN: 1890515019. Lizzie and Ben help the homeless lady who lives down the street in a cardboard box.

Mochizuki, Ken. 1995. *Heroes.* New York: Lee & Low Books. ISBN: 1880000504. A Japanese American boy asks his father and uncle to help him get away from the role of the bad guy he is forced to play in the war games he plays with his friends.

Sacks, Margaret. 1989. *Beyond Safe Boundaries*. New York: Puffin. ISBN: 0140344071. A coming-of-age story that takes place in the 1960s in South Africa when a girl's older sister joins a secret group who opposes the country's racial problems.

Smith, D. 2002. *If the World Were a Village: A Book About the World's People*. Tonawanda, NY: Kids Can Press. ISBN: 1550747797. A wonderful book that compares the world to a village with one hundred citizens. All kinds of facts based on that comparison are shared, such as languages, populations, and foods.

Woodson, Jacqueline. 1995 *Melanin Sun*. New York: The Blue Sky Press. ISBN: 0590458817. Melanin Sun discovers girls and hangs out with his best friend. His mother is involved with a white woman. This book is both a Newberry and Jane Addams Award Winner.

———. 2000. *Miracle's Boys*. New York: G. P. Putnam's Sons. ISBN: 0399231137. A boy's close relationship with his older brother changes after the brother is released from a detention home and blames the younger brother for their mother's death.

Vigna, J. 1995. *My Two Uncles*. Morton Grove, IL: Albert Witman & Company. ISBN: 080755507X. Elly loves her two uncles and can't understand why they are both not invited to her grandparents' fiftieth anniversary.

Violence

Bunting, Eve. 1998. *Your Move*. San Diego, CA: Harcourt Brace. ISBN: 01520001816. When ten-year-old James' gang initiation endangers his six-year-old brother, they find the courage to say, "Thanks, but no thanks."

Loftis, C. 1997. *The Boy Who Sat by the Window: Helping Children Cope with Violence*. Far Hills, NJ: New Horizon Press. ISBN: 0882821474. Joshua reacts to the death of his friend in a random drive-by shooting. Encouraging peace rather than violence is a theme of the book.

MacDonald, Margaret. 1992. *Peace Tales, World Folktales to Talk About*. North Haven, CT: The Shoe String Press. ISBN: 020802328. Stories about peace, war, stubbornness, conflict, and choice.

Rodriguez, Luis J. 1999. *It Doesn't Have to Be This Way: A Barrio Story*. New York: Children's Book Press. ISBN: 0892391618. Written both in Spanish and English. The story of a reluctant boy becoming more and more involved in the activities of a local gang, until a tragic event involving his cousin forces him to make a choice about the course of life.

Shange, Ntozake. 1997. *Whitewash*. New York: Walker Publishing Company. ISBN: 0802784909. A young African American girl is traumatized when a gang attacks her and her brother on their way home from school and spray paints her face white.

Soto, G. 1997. *Buried Onions*. New York: Harcourt Brace Company. ISBN: 0152013334. Eddie, a young Mexican American boy, is trying to make a life in Fresno. His aunt and friends want him to avenge his father, best friend, and cousins' deaths.

Walter, Virginia. 1998. *Making Up Megaboy*. New York: DK Publishing. ISBN: 789424886. When thirteen-year-old Robbie shoots an old man in a liquor store, everyone who knows the quiet, withdrawn youth struggles to understand this act of violence from their own point of view.

Professional Books

Beane, A. 1999. *Bully Free Classroom*. Minneapolis, MN: Free Spirit Publishing. ISBN: 1575420546.

Fine, E., A. Lacey and J. Baer. 1995. *Children as Peacemakers*. Portsmouth, NH: Heinemann. ISBN: 0435088513.

Grapes, B. J. (ed.) 2000. *School Violence*. San Diego, CA: Greenhaven Press. ISBN: 0737703326.

Henkin, R. 1998. *Who's Invited to Share: Using Literacy to Teach for Equity and Social Justice*. Portsmouth, NH: Heinemann. ISBN: 0325000522.

Pierce, K. (ed.) 2000. *Adventuring with Books: A Booklist for PreK–Grade 6*. Urbana, IL: NCTE. ISBN: 0814100775.

Pipher, M. 1994. *Reviving Ophelia: Saving the Selves of Adolescent Girls*. New York: Ballentine Books. ISBN: 0345392825.

Shandler, S. 1999. *Ophelia Speaks*. New York: HarperCollins. ISBN: 0060952970.

Simmons, R. 2002. *Odd Girl Out: The Hidden Culture of Aggression in Girls*. New York: A Harvest Book, Harcourt. ISBN: 0151006040.

Stern-LaRosa, C., and E. Bettman. 2000. *Hate Hurts: How Children Learn and Unlearn Prejudice. A Guide for Adults and Children*. New York: Scholastic. ISBN: 0439211212.

Tatum, B. 1997. *"Why Are All the Black Kids Sitting Together in the Cafeteria?" and Other Conversations About Race*. New York: Basic Books. ISBN: 046509127.

Vasquez, V. 2003. *Negotiating Critical Literacies with Young Children*. Mahwah, NJ: Lawrence Erlbaum. ISBN: 0805840532.

Wiseman, R. 2002. *Queen Bees and Wannabes: Helping Your Daughter Survive Cliques, Gossip, Boyfriends, and Other Realities of Adolescence*. New York: Crown Publishing Group. ISBN: 1400047927.

Yokota, J. (ed.) 2001. *Kaleidoscope: A Multicultural Booklist for Grades K–8*. Urbana, IL: NCTE. ISBN: 0814125409.

Appendix C

Additional Resources

Websites

www.antibullying.net

The Antibullying Network comes from Scotland; it disseminates many ideas about bullying in schools and how it can be tackled.

www.wcwonline.org/bullying/index.html

The Project on Teasing and Bullying is part of the Wellesley Centers for Women. The website describes the project's goals, activities, and training.

www.passion-4.net/bullying/index.shtml

This is a list of the one hundred bullying websites on the Internet.

www.gold.ac.uk/tmr/reports/aim2_firenze1.html

A December 1999 theoretical paper on bullying is posted here.

www.angelfire.com/bc2/hamed

This website is dedicated to the memory of Hamed Nastoh, a fourteen-year-old eighth grader who committed suicide to escape bullying at his school. Its purpose is to promote greater tolerance and respect and thus ensure a better world.

www.dontlaugh.org

This is the Operation Respect: Don't Laugh at Me site. It was founded by Peter Yarrow, of Peter, Paul, and Mary. It's dedicated to fighting ridicule, bullying, and violence. Teachers can register and receive complimentary copies of the curriculum, which include a CD and video. Two programs are available: one for students in grades 2–5, the other for students in grades 6–8.

www.lgcsc.org/robkirkland/mumstory.html

This website is in memory of Robbie Kirkland, who committed suicide at age fourteen. He was bullied because he was gay.

www.womedia.org

This website promotes the extraordinary films Debra Chasnoff has created for teachers and parents. The following films are especially helpful for confronting bullying and name-calling among children:

1. *Let's Get Real.* This film focuses on name-calling and bullying among sixth- through ninth-grade students. It is presented from the students' perspectives and could encourage many discussions about bullying and ways to fight it.

2. *That's a Family.* Children in many different kinds of families talk about their rich diversity. The film helps to dispel stereotypes that children may face.

3. *It's Elementary: Talking About Gay Issues in School.* Students in elementary and middle school classrooms learn to have respect for all kinds of people. The film helps teachers imagine how to develop a more inclusive curriculum by combating stereotypes, derogatory name-calling, and harassment.

www.colorado.edu/cspv/safeschools/bullying/overview.html

This site describes Colorado's Bullying Prevention Program. The Colorado Department of Education summarizes the Colorado bill that requires schools to have bullying prevention and education.

www.glsen.org

This important organization has many materials and resources available to help teachers and students fight bullying, especially for gay, lesbian, bisexual, and transgendered (and those perceived to be) children and families.

www.splcenter.org

The Southern Poverty Law Center is another important organization that is dedicated to fighting injustice and intolerance. They have many resources available. "Ten Ways to Fight Hate: A Community Response Guide" is a wonderful and helpful publication that explores hate and gives specific suggestions for fighting it.

www.gold.ac.uk/euconf

This site is devoted to the European Conference on Initiatives to Combat School Bullying. Keynote addresses are included, and many European countries are represented.

www.opheliaproject.org

The Ophelia Project is dedicated to creating safe schools for girls; it focuses on relational aggression that girls often confront.

www.bullybeware.com/moreinfo.html

Bully B'ware Productions is located in British Columbia, Canada. Information on safe schools, bullying, and successful antibullying campaigns is provided.

www.nea.org

Under "NEA and the issues," click on "school safety," where there is a link to "bullying and harassment." The National Education Association has a National Bullying Awareness Campaign. Information and resources are provided.

www.ncte.org

This is the website for The National Council of Teachers of English. This important literacy organization has many statements, resources, and publications related to the teaching of reading and writing at all levels. The 1999 NCTE Resolution on Diversity is a model for including all children in our literacy classrooms.

www.readwritethink.org

This wonderful website provides high quality literacy teacher lesson plans. There are even critical literacy lessons that focus on bullying.

www.rethinkingschools.org

Rethinking schools has many materials available to help teach students through critical literacy. (Put "bullying" in the search panel on top.)

Photo Exhibit

Love Makes a Family: Living in Gay and Lesbian Families is a photo and text exhibit (photographs by Gigi Kaeser and interviews by Pam Brown and Peggy Gillespie). Black-and-white photographs, with accompanying text, show racially diverse gay and lesbian families and family structures. Teacher resource packet available. Contact Family Diversity Projects, P.O. Box 1209, Amherst, MA 01004-1216; (413) 256-0502.

References

American Psychological Association. 1993. "Violence & Youth: Psychology's Response." *Vol. 1: Summary Report of the American Psychological Association on Violence & Youth*. Washington, DC: American Psychological Association.

Atwell, N. 1998. *In the Middle* (2nd ed.). Portsmouth, NH: Heinemann.

Blanco, J. 2003. *Please Stop Laughing at Me*. Avon, MA: Adams Publishing.

Bogdan, Robert C., and Sari Knopp Biklen. 2002. *Qualitative Research for Education: An Introduction to Theories and Methods* (4th ed). New York: Pearson Education.

Boyd, Lizi. 1991. *Bailey the Big Bully*. New York: Puffin.

Bridges, Ruby. 1999. *Through My Eyes*. New York: Scholastic.

Buckel, David. 1999. *Youth Bring Gay Rights Movement to School*. New York: Lambda Legal Defense and Education Fund.

Bunting, Eve. 1995. *Cheyenne Again*. New York: Clarion Books.

———. 1993. *Fly Away Home*. Madison, WI: Turtleback Books.

———. 1998. *Your Move*. San Diego, CA: Harcourt.

Cannon, Janell. 1993. *Stellaluna*. San Diego, CA: Harcourt.

Caseley, Judith. 1989. *Ada Potato*. New York: Greenwillow.

Cazden, C. 1988. *Classroom Discourse: The Language of Teaching and Learning*. Portsmouth, NH: Heinemann.

Christensen, L. 2000. *Reading, Writing, and Rising Up*. Milwaukee, WI: Rethinking Schools.

Cole, Joanna. 1989. *Bully Trouble*. New York: Random House Books for Young Readers.

———. 1990. *Don't Call Me Names*. New York: Random House.

Coles, Robert. 1995. *The Story of Ruby Bridges*. New York: Scholastic.

———. 1998. *The Moral Intelligence of Children*. New York: Plume.

Cooper, Floyd. 1998. *Coming Home: From the Life of Langston Hughes*. New York: Puffin.

Cushman, Doug. 1990. *Camp Big Paw*. New York: Harper & Row.

Davis, B., D. Sumara, and R. Luce-Kapler. 2000. *Engaging Minds: Learning and Teaching in a Complex World*. Mahwah, NJ: Lawrence Erlbaum.

Dr. Suess. 1961. *The Sneetches and Other Stories*. New York: Random House Books for Young Readers.

Duffey, Betsy. 1993. *How to Be Cool in the Third Grade*. New York: Puffin.

Duncan, Lois. 1990. *Wonder Kid Meets the Evil Lunch Snatcher*. New York: Little Brown & Company.

Dworkin, A. 2000. *Scapegoat*. New York: The Free Press.

Finn, P. and T. McNeil. 1987. *The Response of the Criminal Justice System to Bias Crime: An Exploratory View*. Washington, DC: US Department of Justice.

Glesne, C. 1999. *Becoming Qualitative Researchers*. New York: Addison Wesley Longman.

Graves, D. 1994. *A Fresh Look at Writing*. Portsmouth, NH: Heinemann.

Halperin, I. 1999. *Valediction*. Unpublished manuscript.

Hazler, Richard. 1996. *Breaking the Cycle of Violence: Interventions for Bullying and Victimization*. Washington, DC: Accelerated Development.

Henkin, Roxanne. 1998. *Who's Invited to Share? Using Literacy to Teach for Equity and Social Justice*. Portsmouth, NH: Heinemann.

Hovelsrud, Joyce. 1997. "Young Ladies Don't Slay Dragons." In *Elements of Literature, First Course*. New York: Holt, Rinehart, and Winston.

Howe, James. 1996. *Pinky and Rex and the Bully*. New York: Atheneum.

Innocenti, Roberto. 1985. *Rose Blanche*. Mankato, MN: Creative Education Inc.

Janks, Hilary. 2001. "Identity & Conflict in the Critical Literacy Classroom." In *Negotiating Critical Literacies in Classrooms*, edited by Barbara Comber and Anne Simpson. Mahwah, NJ: Lawrence Erlbaum.

Johnson, J. 1999. *How Do I Feel About Bullies and Gangs?* London: The Watts Publishing Group.

Johnston, Marianne. 1998. *Dealing with Bullying.* New York: Powerkids Press.

———. 2001. *Journal of American Medical Association* (285) 16: 2096–98.

Keene, Ellin and Susan Zimmerman. 1997. *Mosaic of Thought: Teaching Comprehension in a Reader's Workshop.* Portsmouth, NH: Heinemann.

Knight, Margy Burns. 1993. *Who Belongs Here? An American Story.* Gardiner, ME: Tilbury House.

Kovalik, Susan (ed.). 2000. *Tools for Citizenship and Life Using the ITI Lifelong Guidelines and LIFESKILLS in Your Classroom* (2nd ed.) Kent, WA: Kovalik & Associates.

Krensky, Stephen. 1998. *Louise Takes Charge.* New York: Dial Books for Young Readers.

LeDoux, Joseph. 1996. *The Emotional Brain: The Mysterious Underpinnings of Emotional Life.* New York: Touchstone.

Lerner, G. 1997. *Why History Matters: Life and Thought.* New York: Oxford University Press.

Lester, Helen. 2002. *Hooway for Wadney Wat.* New York: Houghton Mifflin.

Livingston, Myra Cohn. 1994. *Keep on Singing: A Ballad of Marian Anderson.* Bridgewater, NJ: Holiday House.

———. 1992. *Let Freedom Ring: A Ballad of Martin Luther King, Jr.* Bridgewater, NJ: Holiday House.

Luke, A., and P. Freebody. 1999. "A Map of Possible Practices: Further Notes on the Four Resources Model." *Practically Primary* 4 (2): 5–8.

Miles, M., and M. Huberman. 1994. *Qualitative Data Analysis.* Thousand Oaks, CA: Sage Publications.

Miller, A. 1990. *For Your Own Good: Hidden Cruelty in Child-Rearing and the Roots of Violence.* New York: Farrar, Straus, Giroux.

———. 2001. *The Truth Will Set You Free: Overcoming Emotional Blindness and Finding Your True Adult Self.* New York: Basic Books.

Nabozny v. Podlesny. No. 95-C-0086-S. Court Records including February 2, 1996, 7th Circuit, December 18, 1995, and Decision July 31, 1996, U.S. Court of Appeals, 7th Circuit 92 F.3d 446.

Nansel, T., M. Overpeck, R. Pilla, W. Ruan, B. Simons-Morton, and P. Scheidt. 2001. "Bullying Behaviors Among US Youth: Prevalence and Association with Psychosocial Adjustment." *Journal of the American Medical Association* (285) 16: 2049–156.

Naylor, Phyllis Reynolds. 1994. *The King of the Playground*. New York: Aladdin Library.

Oram, Hiawyn. 1993. *Angry Arthur*. New York: Random House Children's Books.

Parks, Rosa. 1999. *I Am Rosa Parks*. New York: Puffin.

Passen, Lisa. 1991. *Fat, Fat, Rose Marie*. New York: Henry Holt & Company.

Petty, Kate. 1991. *Being Bullied*. New York: Barrons Juveniles.

Philbrick, Rodman. 1999. *Freak the Mighty*. New York: Econo-Clad Books.

Polacco, Patricia. 1998. *My Rotten Redheaded Older Brother*. New York: Simon & Schuster Books for Young Readers.

———. 1998. *Thank You Mr. Falker*. New York: Philomel Books.

Pollack, W. 1998. *Real Boys: Rescuing Our Sons from the Myths of Boyhood*. New York: Henry Holt & Co.

Poulet, Virginia, and Donald Charles. 1971. *Blue Bug and the Bullies*. Danbury, CT: Children's Press.

Powell, Jillian. 1999. *Talking About Bullying*. New York: Raintree/ Steck Vaughn.

Ringgold, Faith. 1995. *Aunt Harriet's Underground Railroad in the Sky*. New York: Dragonfly.

———. 1996. *Dinner at Aunt Connie's House*. New York: Hyperion.

———. 1998. *My Dream of Martin Luther King*. New York: Dragonfly.

Rodriguez, Luis J. 1999. *It Doesn't Have to Be This Way: A Barrio Story*. New York: Children's Book Press.

Romain, Trevor. 1997. *Bullies Are a Pain in the Brain*. Minneapolis, MN: Free Spirit Publishing.

Rosenblatt, Louise M. 1978. *The Reader the Text the Poem: The Transactional Theory of the Literary Work*. Carbondale, IL: Southern Illinois University Press.

Sanders, Pete. 1997. *Let's Talk About Feeling Safe*. New York: Ramboro Books PLC.

Sanders, P., and S. Myers. 2000. *What Do You Know About Bullying?* New York: Franklin Watts.

Sautter, R. Craig. 1995. "Standing Up to Violence." *Phi Delta Kappan*, January. K1–K12.

Short, K., J. Harste, and C. Burke. 1996. *Creating Classrooms for Authors and Inquirers* (2nd ed.). Portsmouth, NH: Heinemann.

Simmons, Rachel. 2002. *Odd Girl Out.* New York: Harper.

Smith, Karen. 1995. "Bringing Children and Literature Together in the Elementary Classroom." *Primary Voices*, K–6 3 (2): 22–32.

Spear, Karen. 1988. *Sharing Writing: Peer Response Groups in English Classes.* Portsmouth, NH: Boynton/Cook.

Spradley, James. 1979. *The Ethnographic Interview.* New York: Holt, Rinehart & Winston.

Svoboda, Elizabeth. 2004. "Everybody Loves a Bully: Middle School Tormentors Win the Popularity Contest." *Psychology Today*, March/April: 20.

Taylor, M. 1991. *Let the Circle Be Unbroken.* New York: Puffin Books.

———. 1991. *"Roll of Thunder, Hear My Cry."* New York: Scholastic.

Thomas, Pat, and Lesley Harker. 2000. *Stop Picking on Me: A First Look at Bullying.* New York: Barron's Educational Series.

Walter, Virginia. 1998. *Making Up Megaboy.* New York: DK Publishing, Inc.

Weiss, Gerry. 2002. "Gay Teen to get $312,000 Settlement." *Erie Times News*, January 17.

Wilhelm, Hans. 2001. *Tyrone the Horrible.* New York: Scholastic.

Wilson, Lorraine. 2002. *Reading to Live: How to Teach Reading for Today's World.* Portsmouth, NH: Heinemann.

Winthrop, Elizabeth. 1992. *Luke's Bully.* New York: Puffin.

Zemelman, S., and H. Daniels. 1988. *A Community of Writers: Teaching Writing in the Junior and Senior High School.* Portsmouth, NH: Heinemann.